ROCKHOUNDING
Idaho

Help Us Keep This Guide Up to Date

Every effort has been made by the author and editors to make this guide as accurate and useful as possible. However, many things can change after a guide is published—trails are rerouted, regulations change, techniques evolve, facilities come under new management, and so forth.

We appreciate hearing from you concerning your experiences with this guide and how you feel it could be improved and kept up to date. While we may not be able to respond to all comments and suggestions, we'll take them to heart and we'll also make certain to share them with the author. Please send your comments and suggestions to the following address:

FalconGuides
Reader Response/Editorial Department
246 Goose Lane
Guilford, CT 06437

Thanks for your input, and happy rockhounding!

ROCKHOUNDING
Idaho

A Guide to 99 of the State's Best Rockhounding Sites

Second Edition

GARRET ROMAINE

FALCONGUIDES

GUILFORD, CONNECTICUT

To my mother, Carol, who handed down her love for the written word

FALCONGUIDES®

An imprint of The Rowman & Littlefield Publishing Group, Inc.
4501 Forbes Blvd., Ste. 200
Lanham, MD 20706
www.rowman.com
Falcon and FalconGuides are registered trademarks and Make Adventure Your Story is a trademark of The Rowman & Littlefield Publishing Group, Inc.

Distributed by NATIONAL BOOK NETWORK

Copyright © 2010 The Rowman & Littlefield Publishing Group, Inc.
This FalconGuides edition 2020
Photos by Garret Romaine unless otherwise noted
Maps by The Rowman & Littlefield Publishing Group, Inc.

British Library Cataloguing-in-Publication Information Available

Library of Congress Cataloging-in-Publication Data available

ISBN 978-1-4930-3411-6 (paper: alk. paper)
ISBN 978-1-4930-3412-3 (electronic)

∞™ The paper used in this publication meets the minimum requirements of American National Standard for Information Sciences—Permanence of Paper for Printed Library Materials, ANSI/NISO Z39.48-1992.

The author and The Rowman & Littlefield Publishing Group, Inc., assume no liability for accidents happening to, or injuries sustained by, readers who engage in the activities described in this book.

CONTENTS

Overview

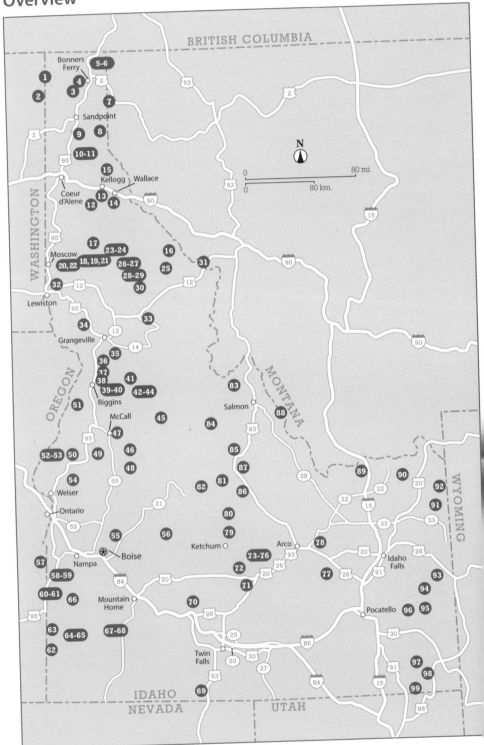

Contents **vii**

PREFACE

This update includes field work up to summer 2019. There are still several confusing situations surrounding some of the best rockhounding locales in Idaho, so I want to emphasize that conditions in the field are always in flux. Land use designations change, mining claims come and go, and the relentless approach of development can alter things overnight. I can't stress enough the importance of joining a local rock and gem club, frequenting a local rock shop, and networking for more up-to-date information.

Some very large parcels of land in Idaho are off-limits to rockhounding. These areas include Indian reservations, wilderness areas, federal energy development areas, and, of course, private land. Fortunately, there is also a lot of public land in Idaho. USDA Forest Service (USFS) and Bureau of Land Management (BLM) holdings take up about two-thirds of the state.

Despite my best efforts to find all the best spots, I'm sure I left a few discoveries for future explorers. I added information about additional opportunities throughout the text, but I undoubtedly missed a few. Nevertheless, if anyone were to systematically charge through every single site listed here, the result would be a complete and representative collection of the best of Idaho's gems, rocks, minerals, metals, and fossils.

Your trips will be successful if you plan ahead and be prepared. Whether you drive a loop and eventually head back home or zip through a section of Idaho and hope for a few souvenirs, the information here gets the job done. You can set up a base camp and make repeated sorties in all directions, or you can hunker down in some premier spots for several days. Remember that the longer a spot is listed in a guidebook, the more likely it is that you may need to get off the beaten track to find what you're looking for. Idaho is a great state to roam and explore; most important—have fun out there.

ACKNOWLEDGMENTS

Nobody should have to rockhound alone. It has been my pleasure to cover the state of Idaho with a dedicated team of helpers, who supported me with their skills at camping, hiking, cooking, navigating, and cooler care. In the hope of securing their attendance for future expeditions, I want to take the space to thank them by name: neighborhood friends Jake and Kyle Riley; trusted scout Dirk Williams; and my soapstone buddy, Marty Schippers. My family has been great, including my late father, Garret Lee; my late uncle Doug Romaine; my cousin John Romaine and his young son, Douglas; and, most importantly, my long-suffering wife, Cindy, who helps with the driving and occasionally lets me rockhound till dark.

Rachel Houghton provided an editing sanity check and helped with photography tools in the first edition. Tony Griffin, then president of the Idaho Gem Club, provided assistance in the early years and helped me track down a few wayward sites. Tim Fisher provided expert guidance as well. I thank you all.

Most of all, I want to acknowledge you, the reader. Thanks for helping to keep one of the oldest hobbies going, and thanks for whatever you end up passing down to the next generation. I've met a lot of nice people while out rockhounding in Idaho; and I think you will too.

INTRODUCTION

Every guidebook includes a lot of background information in the front and back. This one follows that template. If you're an experienced camper and longtime outdoors-type person, steeped in the ways of collecting but new to much of Idaho, you can skim through a lot of this introduction. If, in addition, you already have experience with Idaho rockhounding, you can skip even more and go right to the locales. I offer information, warnings, and guidelines here for safety compliance and as a way to welcome anyone new to the hobby.

Idaho's Geology

The geological forces that shaped Idaho are complex and include at least five key events:

1. The deposition and hardening of the great Belt Series, a large zone of Precambrian and Cambrian sediments occupying much of the Panhandle.
2. The emplacement of the Idaho Batholith and related stocks such as the Kaniksu and Atlanta Batholiths. These granites intruded during the Mesozoic and make up the mountainous central region. They are very prominent.
3. The birth of the Rocky Mountains added metamorphism and elevation, pushing up large blocks of older rock.
4. A giant hot spot created the basalt plains, typified by Craters of the Moon, and is now beneath the Yellowstone Caldera. The basalt flows were accompanied by ash beds and lava tubes.
5. Basin and range faulting, common throughout many of the western states, is spreading from the south.

Idaho is known as the Gem State thanks to those granite batholiths. As granite stocks push their way up through the older basement rocks, they melt or grind up rocks in their way. Pure granite is made up of silica and feldspars and other simple minerals, which freeze up first as the granite cools. Once all the "normal" material is locked up, there is often a "remainder" still circulating at the edges of the granite mass. This hot, quartz-rich solution can carry exotic material such as metals and sulfides. Idaho has witnessed many great gold rushes and stampedes into the mountains because the edges of the granite stocks are often shot through with big quartz veins. If cooling occurs at a slow, steady rate, even more interesting crystallization results, leading to pegmatite gems such as smoky quartz, topaz, sapphire, ruby, mica, beryl, and garnet. Simply put, you can never get tired of Idaho's granite.

Rockhounding in Idaho

Most of Idaho's top collecting locales have been known for decades. After World War II, a generation of weekend adventurers scoured US public lands for rocks and minerals. Gas was cheap, cars were big and powerful, and many small towns supported their own rock shops. In the intervening years, those well-known sites were hit hard. By 2008 most of the local rock shops were closed and many popular sites were either completely cleaned out except for a few small chips or locked up on private lands, valid mineral claims, reservations, wilderness areas, or critical habitats, restricted and regulated to the brink of elimination. Many more rock shops have closed over the ensuing years, but the hobby endures.

If we found that an old site is now closed, wiped out, questionable, or off-limits, we noted it wherever necessary. We worked hard to find a few of the more obscure historic sites, such as the ones described in Beckwith's 1972 book or in Eckert's vague listings (see bibliography). I know a few landowners will be grateful that new information is being published. I heard one story about a rancher who was greeted by a rockhound coming up to his door, guidebook in hand. "That book!" the rancher lamented. "I've had folks coming to the door for years, and there ain't nothin' out there!"

In the interest of erring on the side of good rockhounding, I included three sites that are technically in another state but less than 2 miles across the Idaho border. These sites are among my favorites, so I blurred the lines a little for Graveyard Point plume agate (Oregon), Solo Creek quartz crystals (Washington), and Lolo Pass smoky quartz (Montana). In all three cases, access is primarily from the Idaho direction.

From my own experience, there are four main ways to use a rockhounding guidebook:

1. Planning out destination camps where you can hunker down and truly explore a significant area, using sorties and mini-loops as necessary. The camping, hiking, fishing, and photography will be excellent, and you won't be packing up every morning.
2. Creating small loops that string together a series of locales over a long weekend or more, with one or more good sites per day, and usually including at least one "top ten" spot. You stay on the move, see a lot of country, and really get to know a region.

3. Checking each spot off methodically, in turn, and completing the entire state list from top to bottom—perhaps in one year or season. Rockhounding on steroids, in other words.
4. Finding you are in (or going through) an area or region and wondering if there is anything at least close or on the way. Desperation and efficiency practically ensure success.

Noncollecting but Geology-Related Opportunities

In addition to the listed rockhounding areas, Idaho has several touring, viewing, and educational opportunities with a geological bent but no collecting. Bring your camera. Craters of the Moon National Monument is a fantastic walk through recent lava fields. The Hagerman Fossil Beds National Monument is fascinating, and hopefully someday the museum will expand from its cramped little storefront. Soda Springs, located on the Oregon Trail, is no Old Faithful, but it's a good warm-up if you're headed through Idaho to Yellowstone National Park. The Tolo Lake Mammoth Site is a worthwhile stop along US 95 near Grangeville, and Hells Canyon is a must-see.

Idaho has hot springs, dunes, alpine lakes, and countless old mining camps and abandoned mines. Try to combine some standard tourism with your rockhounding to come away with a true appreciation for the state, or to keep the less-rabid rockhounds in the car occupied. Many other books, especially FalconGuides, stand ready to guide you through noncollecting opportunities such as hiking, mountain biking, hot springs soaking, etc. My job here is to talk about rocks.

Top Ten Rockhounding Sites

If I wanted to impress someone new to rockhounding with only the most productive, guaranteed fantastic places in Idaho, here's where I'd go, starting at the northern end and then down and hooking roughly east:

Emerald Creek for star garnets
Fossil Bowl for leaf fossils
Cuprum for copper ores
Graveyard Point for plume agate
Bruneau River for tumbler material
Rabbit Springs for thundereggs
Salmon River at Yankee Fork, East Fork, and main stem for gold, garnet, jasper, agate, and petrified wood

Challis area for fluorite and more

Leaton Gulch, also near Challis, for meteorite impact breccia

Spencer Opal Mines

The sites included in this book vary in quality. I admit my standards can be pretty diverse when it comes to simple rockhounding. I enjoy a good long hike across a gravel bar—I'll grid it off in my head and search the whole thing. I can still make a decent sagebrush scramble, but I sometimes get distracted by flowers and animal tracks. I am constantly amazed at being able to pan a few colors of gold just about everywhere in the old districts, and I try to bring back a little black sand every time I go into the gold country. The older I get, the more I appreciate settling in and digging all day at a fossil-rich outcrop. All those enthusiasms are baked into this book.

I hope you find a quiet place that you can call your own favorite spot in Idaho and build your personal top-ten list. When you have a lot of the state to explore for the first time, it's tempting to keep going to new areas. My advice is to mix it up a little—sometimes you need to slow down at a single spot for a couple nights; sometimes you need to go back and try again.

Gold Prospecting

Every rockhound is a little different. Other than true generalists, most of us have a favorite material to seek out, be it gold, gems, fossils, or semiprecious stones. After geology school, I started gold prospecting as a serious hobby, and my dream site is an old lode mine with a nice nearby creek to pan in, some picturesque buildings to photograph, and a vast tailings pile to explore. Throw in some fossils and plentiful firewood, and you've got Mineral, Idaho.

For those of you eager to try your hand searching for gold, Idaho should put a smile on your face. The old-time miners skimmed off a lot of the easy pickings, and the Chinese teams got a lot of the hard stuff. Depression-era miners later found a little bit more, and electronic prospectors using metal detectors have done well recently. But nobody can get it all. Every big storm can improve collecting, and each spring flood stirs up the gravels to some degree. The trick is to keep practicing and dig deep holes. As you collect more and more concentrates, learn to read them with a hand lens.

Many excellent specimens are still found on tailings piles abandoned as worthless years ago. Remote mining camps sometimes faced prohibitive shipping fees, and in some cases good ore never left the mine site. Elsewhere, tailings were rich enough to reprocess at a second profit. Until you look around and check, you never can predict what you might find. Just know the land status by searching for posted signs, be on the lookout for recent claim markers, and stay safe.

Community Pits

The BLM has a great program in Idaho that allows the public to purchase mass quantities of river rock, pebbles, flagstone, cinders, and other material. These community pits are reasonably priced—such as 90 cents per cubic yard for basalt and riprap at Spar Canyon. Owyhee, Bruneau, Shoshone, and Pocatello also have community pits. If you live in or near one of those BLM districts, you should check them out.

Best References

After this book, there are two must-have references for collecting geological specimens in Idaho: Lanny Ream's latest effort, the first edition of *Gem Trails of Idaho and Western Montana,* and the most up-to-date version of Tim Fisher's *Ore-Rock-On* DVD (now also available on USB drives and SD cards). Ream is an excellent mineralogist and field geologist, and he has collected more Idaho gem locales than anyone else I know. Fisher, also an excellent rockhound who is particularly good with fossils, lists almost 3,000 GPS coordinates for rocks, minerals, and fossils in the Pacific Northwest, but many of his Idaho locales remain unverified. I reported on as many as I could so that he can update his records. Incidentally, both Ream and Fisher are still actively field collecting, and they show up periodically on organized trips.

The more research you can do before an outing, the better your odds of success. I've listed a few books, papers, and pamphlets in the bibliography, and more old papers are coming online each year. To dive deep into Idaho's riches, you'll need to research state and federal geology bulletins, graduate theses, mine reports, and more. Join a local club and start asking questions. Any time you plan to hit a spot long and hard, I'd recommend that you do as much research as you can.

Collecting Regulations and Etiquette

There are a lot of restrictions, controversies, and limitations you should know about as a beginning rockhound. (Experienced collectors can skip all this, including my admitted rants that follow.)

Collecting is not allowed in national parks or monuments.

For example, it is a little-known fact to beginning collectors that the federal government puts a limit of 25 pounds and one piece per day per person for obsidian and petrified wood. In a year, you're restricted to 250 pounds total. It's a hobby, not a job—leave some for the next crew. You'll know when you're ready for commercial quantities.

You aren't allowed to collect vertebrate fossils from public land, period. That's anything with a backbone, if you remember your high school biology. No reptiles, no mammals, no birds, no fish, and no amphibians. If you want to do that kind of collecting, you must join the right organization to secure the proper permits. Leaves and trees and shells are currently fine, although you never know what new laws are in store. Personally, I think restrictions on fossil hunting are ridiculous. Here's an example: Say I find a 50-pound gold nugget the size of a basketball—it would be worth maybe a half-million dollars. Unless I was somewhere I didn't belong, that nugget is mine. Ditto for a garnet the size of my head. Now, say I am out in some Eocene ash beds on public land and I stumble across a fossil horse like those at Hagerman. At most it would be worth $10,000 or $15,000 once it was excavated, cleaned, prepared, and mounted, which can take years. But without the right permits, the fossil stays in the ground, to erode away in the rain and wind. Naturally I'd tell someone in a position to collect it, but that person might not have time. In fact, many museums are already bulging at the seams with tray after tray of fossil material, while some have boxes in storage that haven't been cleaned or cataloged. At the same time, erosion and natural forces are wiping out fossils in the field every day. Better, I would think, for dedicated amateurs to get out there and sleuth. The more good fossils rescued from erosion, the better.

Archaeology is another sore topic. As a rockhound, you are allowed to pick up agate, jasper, and obsidian. As we know, these materials were often used to make arrowheads, knives, scrapers, hatchets, and spear points. You aren't allowed to go out searching specifically for arrowheads and other tools, but in the course of your rockhounding in dry washes and gulches, you may frequently come across chips that *might* be broken arrowheads or cutting tools—it's hard to tell after they've been tumbled in the gravels of a river or creek, broken half beyond recognition and coated with mud. You're allowed to pick these up, in most cases, unless you're in a restricted artifact area (such as the one along the east side of the Bruneau River), but you can't sell them.

A government archaeologist from Wyoming once told me that there are specific exclusions in the Antiquities Act (as revised some time ago) that preclude sanctions on casual rockhounds. The law does not seek to punish those who surface collect on public lands and "accidentally" find material. I want to believe him, but I've never been able to get corroborating testimony. I put in several requests to then US Senator Orrin Hatch's office, as he was suggested as the lawmaker who wrote into the act the stipulation that rockhounds could still pick up flakes and chips of agate, jasper, etc., but the office never got back to me.

One thing is certain, however: You cannot, under any circumstances, dig or screen for artifacts on public land. That's illegal, immoral, and just bad manners. Be a good prospector, and leave such work to trained archaeologists. Pot hunters have a deservedly bad reputation—one step above grave robbers.

Idaho has rich archaeological resources.

Then there are treasure laws. If you discover a great coin hoard, the competing jurisdictions can be maddening. In Europe, there are official rules that split the value fifty-fifty between the landowner and the finder, with a state museum as the buyer. In Idaho, as across the United States, there is no telling what would happen with a great metal detector find.

My final gripe is the status of Idaho's wilderness areas. There are several historic collecting areas in the Sawtooth Wilderness Area, where collectors had long extracted aquamarine and other exotic material from productive vugs and cavities. Supposedly, those activities were not suspended when the wilderness designation was bestowed on the Sawtooths. However, all collecting in that Idaho wilderness is now forbidden.

Mining Claims

There are countless old scare stories and tall tales about claim jumpers getting shot by gun-toting madmen who resembled Yosemite Sam. There was certainly a time in a few Wild West camps when claim jumping was a serious health risk, but usually attorneys are involved today. Don't be stymied over fears of drawing fire in the middle of a good spot. The legal act of mineral trespass is specific— you have to be purposefully trying to rip someone off by wantonly extracting the good stuff from their well-marked claim. Walking across a mineral claim is not illegal. Owning the mineral rights to a piece of public land does not preclude, for example, anyone with a valid fishing license from fishing there.

Patented land, which started out as a valid mining claim and then became private property, is invariably posted and usually fenced. You're not likely to accidentally trespass; usually, you have to climb fences or ignore postings to get into trouble. Climbing a posted fence is always a sure sign of trouble, so don't do it.

An innocent mistake is not likely to get you into hot water. It is the claim holder's responsibility to take the necessary steps to avoid the likelihood of someone inadvertently going to work on a current claim. Valid mining claims are to be marked with corner posts, and one post should bear the official papers stating the name of the claim, the claim holder, a county clerk's signature and date, and so forth. You are certainly allowed to review such information if you can find it. I've learned that it's productive to actually chat with claim owners on the spot. They tend to be very knowledgeable about local conditions, and may even invite you to dip a pan, if for no other reason than to critique your technique.

Over the years, I've learned to spot claim markers without leaving the car. You start to look for hand-painted signs on big trees, and you pick up a knack for spying those white polyvinyl chloride (PVC) pipes driven into the ground. If there are a lot of claims in an area, that means it was good once. The truth is that just because you see a sign doesn't mean it's a current claim. Claim holders are supposed to take down old markers, but they often don't get around to it once their paperwork lapses. It costs money to carry a claim year after year, and marginal claims frequently expire. The BLM's claims database can screen for expired claims, and you should learn how to use it if you are doing serious exploration.

The point is that some of the areas I have listed here are likely to change legal status over the years. As the price of gold hovers around $1,500 per ounce (at this writing), the guess is that a few new precious metals claims will get staked. But you never know: Some upcoming global calamity may someday push gold prices to $5,000 per ounce. If so, you can expect to dodge a lot more claims out there, especially in the Boise Basin. But if the price drops back to $500 per ounce, more areas will certainly open up.

Tribal Land

Don't even bother trying to collect material on an Indian reservation unless it is in the right-of-way, such as at Cottonwood. Unless you are yourself a Native American, or know one who lives there, chances are slim that you will gain the right to legally collect on tribal land. The only exception is the gravels along the Clearwater River coming into Lewiston. By custom, rockhounds have searched the Clearwater for sillimanite and tumbler material for decades. There are several public access points set up by the BLM along the Clearwater, right off US 12. If collecting is restricted in the future, it will be because rockhounds are getting blamed for littering, trespassing, and/or property damage. Please do your part to prevent more closures. Meanwhile, stay off the reservations. I skipped a promising locale at Tensed and ignored a fossil search near Slickpoo.

Private Land

The US government controls millions of acres of public land, most of which you have every right to set foot on. I suggest you stick to that public land. I have never been very good at going up to people's houses and asking for permission to rockhound on their property. The fossil club I belong to has had tremendous luck in the past at getting access, but my guess is that fossil hunting, being mostly a scientific endeavor, is an easier sell when you're on a family's porch. If someone came up my driveway seeking permission to haul off all the agate and jasper he could find, I'd either say no or make sure I went with him. So avoid private land, and respect property boundaries.

Idaho does a good job of providing recreational access to creeks and rivers.

State Land

Idaho is a friendly state for anglers and hunters. Through a private-public partnership, the state has created the Access Yes! program, which designates considerable acreage for public use, with certain restrictions (you generally can't camp on these lands, for example). Still, the program grants access to many stream and river gravels, and the signs can be extremely welcome when trying to figure out how to get to the water's edge.

Safety and Precautions

Never go into a mine shaft unless you have a lot of safety bases covered. I personally like wheelchair-accessible mine tours, such as in Wallace. Otherwise, you need tools such as the following: lights and extra batteries, a helmet, walkie-talkies, food and water, ropes, tackle, shovels, and hammers. You should know what the heck you're doing, and if you enjoy going into mine shafts, give serious thought to joining a spelunking club or Northwest Underground Explorations (NUE). Never go into a shaft alone, and never go into a shaft with old wooden timbers for shoring or with strange-colored water seeping out of the entrance—that should cover 99 percent of them. Stay safe.

In Idaho, the only shafts I ventured into were in Mineral. They had no timbering and went in only about 20 feet. I peeked in—I could always see daylight, and the adit was hacked out of solid rock. Since I didn't find anything in there, I didn't list coordinates for the mines themselves for that site. Nothing in this book suggests you should ever go into any old mine. Not one collecting locale published here is inside a mine—only the tailings are documented in this book. Every old mining area you visit offers the risk of a cave-in or a fall into an underground tunnel. Be very careful. Never bring young kids or dogs to an old mining area and just turn them loose unsupervised. There are too many rusty nails, broken pieces of glass, rotten timbers, open pits, and jagged pieces of metal out there.

One of my favorite road signs

Never swing a hammer without taking into account what will happen when you break off a piece of rock. Wear safety glasses and gloves at all times when attacking rocks with hammers and chisels, and keep people and pets away. Don't use a hammer meant for driving nails; it can't handle rock that is harder than steel.

Pack up a decent first-aid kit for your car, and know how to use it. At a bare minimum, you should be ready to remove splinters, bandage up cuts, and cover burns. The more times you head outdoors with kids, the more likely you are to treat a bug bite, bee sting, broken bone, or other serious problem. Keep all that in mind as you head out, and be prepared for just about anything.

Seasonal Roads

A rockhound from northern Idaho told me there are three driving seasons in the state: ice, mud, and dust. Another claimed there are two: winter and road construction. Because the mountains are so tall, Idaho's passes can remain snowed in through July. Heavy rain can turn any dirt road into a frightening drive in sloppy mud. Then comes the dust, choking your filters, and finally back to rain again before the snow flies. I've tried to note any special challenges for each locale, but it's hard to anticipate all the problems you can run into. If I can offer one piece of advice, it would be to invest in some excellent tires, because tires seem to find every sharp rock and rusty nail. Then buy an electric air pump and an emergency patch kit. For a few years, kids would drag wooden pallets out to the desert to burn for firewood, leaving behind a black circle full of nails. Fortunately, that practice is losing its luster.

Idaho's back roads contain many hazards, so be very careful.

Wildlife

On one six-day car trip, we counted more than forty deer, one bear, and one moose along the road. That wasn't counting carcasses, of which there were many. Along the Salmon River near Shoup, we saw more sheep than deer. The more you drive, the more likely you are to have an encounter with wildlife. Slow down and be vigilant.

Other wildlife dangers include mountain lions, grizzly bears, rattlesnakes, and yellow jackets. It's a dangerous world out there, and you should always be on the lookout for such hazards. It's best to avoid disturbing these creatures, but chances are, you probably won't see many.

Weather

As the jump-off date for a rockhounding trip approaches, I use internet resources to keep on top of changing weather conditions. Many websites offer fairly decent seven- or ten-day forecasts that should be taken with just a small chunk of halite. Conditions often change quickly, but at least you can be aware of current patterns. At the very least, check the news or listen to the radio as you drive in case a fire has broken out from lightning strikes. Make sure you bring cold-weather gear such as boots, gloves, hat, and coat, plus hot-weather protection such as sunscreen. Play it safe at all times.

Maps

Most hikers and campers can read a map, so I'm not going to go into detail here. My best advice is to get a USFS or BLM map of an area you intend to visit. The newer, the better. Topographical maps are good, but they don't show all the gates and closures; neither does Google Earth. Land status maps do show gates, but be prepared to spend a little money on them.

Not every rockhound needs to know how to read a geology map, but I recommend learning the basics. If you enjoy long hikes for petrified wood and agate, you probably aren't as interested in the bedrock geology of an area until you intend to do some heavy digging. Mineral hunters and gold prospectors find a lot of material in outcrops, and it helps to know what different formations are out there. Ditto for fossil hunters—if you're looking for Cretaceous ammonites, you need to find Cretaceous terrain. Every year, more and more geology maps are finding their way onto the internet as Adobe Acrobat files, and that's a good thing. If you think you don't know how to read a geology map, the basic concept is really simple: different colors for different bedrock. Each color is explained on the map, so it won't take you long to figure out what's going on. Geology has some quirky terms, so search for help on words you don't understand.

GPS Coordinates

The greatest single upgrade for modern prospecting is the handheld Global Positioning System (GPS) unit, but now you can do the same thing with a car-mounted unit or good mobile device. Get one that accepts inputs from your computer, and fill 'er up with waypoints. Once you're in the field, you can drive in close and then guide yourself to within feet of a known spot. I've had some "advisors" tell me that I'm making it too easy for the reader, but I don't agree. I worked hard to collect some of these readings, and I don't want you to make the same mistakes I did. I want you to be successful. A man once found an 80-pound agate in southern Washington by using one of my books as a starting point to sharpen his eye. Believe me—that made my day.

The downside to listing exact GPS coordinates is that a spot I found and published can get virtually wiped out by two or three efficient rockhounding

Map Legend

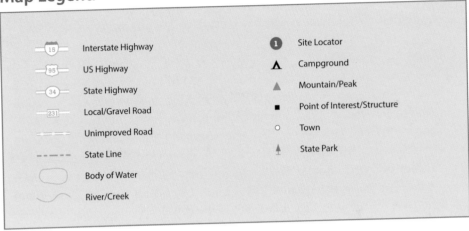

🛣 15 Interstate Highway	① Site Locator
🛣 95 US Highway	▲ Campground
🛣 34 State Highway	▲ Mountain/Peak
🛣 231 Local/Gravel Road	■ Point of Interest/Structure
— — — Unimproved Road	○ Town
– — – — State Line	⚓ State Park
Body of Water	
River/Creek	

parties. I tried to list sites where that wasn't an issue, or I noted it as necessary. In many cases I offer suggestions for further exploration. Sometimes, the farther you can venture from your car, the better off you'll be.

As a longtime consumer of rockhounding guides before I started writing them, I always complained the most about "nonspecific" locales, where the author, usually before the days of accurate handheld GPS units, would have to "punt" on an area. The instructions would describe a likely spot with advice to "check the creek gullies and dry washes over a 10-mile stretch" or something similarly vague. Now that I'm on the other side of the pen, I understand the problems the author faced. Some of the sites in this book also involve exploring, but I'll get you started with exact coordinates.

HOW TO USE THIS BOOK

Each site in this book is accompanied by a host of information. Here's a breakdown.

Land type: This is a terse description of the landforms at the collecting locale. Much of the public land in Idaho is either sagebrush or pine forest, so this information can help for firewood purposes. Many locations involve a creek or river bar, pit, or diggings. Multiple sites can be hard to describe.

County: Identifies the county (or counties) where the site is found, since many older rockhounding guides were organized by county.

GPS: I use a Garmin Nuvi GPS, and my readings are WGS84 standard, with latitude and longitude in decimal format to five places. The readings are easy to paste into Google Earth, without the intricacies of north, south, minutes, and seconds to contend with. All GPS data was verified with Google Earth to avoid suspect readings. GPS coordinates are followed by the site's elevation.

Best season: Rockhounding is meant to be an enjoyable outdoor activity that helps build up your cardiovascular system and strengthen your bones. It isn't meant to be an endurance test while contending with bad weather and forced marches on a billy goat trail. For the most part, mountain passes don't open up until late June, and they can close up again in August in a bad year. Elevations as low as 3,500 feet can be a challenge into late May during cold years. Conversely, desert rockhounding can be tolerable in February with luck and the right gear, but things can get wet and messy in late spring. Some of these sites are on, or close to, pavement, and some require at least hiking to the creek to find a gravel bar. I tried to give a sense for the time of year with the best chance for success. Most creek and river walks yield success only during low water, later in the year. Likewise, serious gold prospecting via dredge is usually restricted until July and ends in early September. So summer months are usually best, at least high up.

Land manager: Most sites are either on USFS or BLM land. The way jurisdictions have coalesced over the years, the districts I've listed may use a different name in the future, so be flexible on that. USFS maps are a great investment, but they require constant updates as new maps are published. Fee-dig sites on private land are noted as such. Road cuts are usually owned by some public agency, and managers hate it when rockhounds leave boulders in their roads and ditches.

Material: This section lists the primary, secondary, and tertiary collectibles at the site as necessary. In cases where the ubiquitous tumbler material contains a unique or noteworthy challenge, I list it. Ditto for black sands; just about every major body of water in Idaho carries magnetite to some extent, and trace gold is common anywhere water drains the Idaho Batholith. Some districts feature an extra ingredient in their concentrates, such as tantalum, iridium, or thorium, to name a few. Elsewhere, you have a fighting chance to identify garnets, sapphires, epidote, corundum, topaz—even diamonds. Just bring a hand lens.

Tools: Most rockhounds have a geology pick, an all-purpose specialty hammer capable of breaking up smaller rocks and chiseling. Picks are also useful for prying half-buried specimens from the soil. To truly explore the geological wonders of Idaho, you'll need a few more tools in your collection. Start with a heavier crack hammer, up to 4 pounds in weight, so you have more authority in your swing. Chisels and gads are great for splitting rocks and taking advantage of cracks and cavities. Typical gold-panning equipment includes two or three pans, some small trowels, a bucket, a screen, and a big shovel. You'll also need multiple sample jars and some kind of suction device, such as an eye dropper, sniffer bottle, or turkey baster, to efficiently suck up the bottom of your gold pan and safely tuck it away in a bottle. A funnel also comes in handy. Invest in screens with at least two different meshes; even a metal noodle drainer from Goodwill does the trick in a pinch.

Vehicle: I know some of you are going to find yourself taking chances with a sedan or minivan out on Idaho's back roads. I wish it weren't so, but it's true. My advice: Don't. Veteran collectors drive a truck, jeep, or SUV with four-wheel drive (4WD), sturdy suspension, 8-ply all-season tires, and air-conditioning. A new breed of collector brings in an ATV (all-terrain vehicle). If your rig isn't up to the task at hand, simply get close, park in a safe spot, and head out on foot. Don't push your vehicle beyond its limits; otherwise, invest in a come-along and a tow chain. Many of these sites are marked "4WD," and that's sometimes charitable on a bad day. Rain, hail, sleet, and snow can ruin an outing fast. Surrender, and come back another day.

Accommodations: Within reason, you can camp on most public lands; ergo, you can spend the night at most of these sites. There are separate books available for the elite RV and trailer crowd, and you folks are probably fine on your own and picky besides. For the next tier of campers, I listed nearby developed campgrounds wherever I could, but be advised that campgrounds can close due to fire, flood, or fiat. For readers who already hunt, fish, hike, bike, or otherwise recreate outdoors, primitive camping, sometimes called "dry camping" (the forest service calls it "dispersed camping"), is a given. Where primitive camping is reasonable, I reported it.

Firewood is usually an issue, so we always brought propane and briquettes just in case. We also collected a lot of dead sagebrush, and burned cow patties more than once. During fire season, you can count on increasing restrictions, so be flexible and know before you go. Always be safe with fire, burn in a sturdy fire pit, and scrape the duff away from the fire ring as much as 10 feet in every direction if at all possible. In our group, we created a legend out of Steve Swartzell, who was religious about clearing anything burnable away from the fire. To "swartzell" became the term for going the extra mile while creating a fire ring. Again, be safe, and know when not to burn.

Special attractions: Special attractions are features close to a certain locale, such as lakes, reservoirs, mines, lodges, and cities. I started with the closest official scenic highway or byway. Most rest areas along the interstate highways offer the opportunity to pick up a copy of the *Idaho Scenic Byways* brochure, as many rockhounding sites begin with a ride on these back roads. Idaho offers an assortment of interesting stops with varying geological ties. Again, there are entire guidebooks for general tourism and related activities, so I didn't go into detail here. My primary duty is to talk about rocks, so most of the special attractions listed are geology-related in some way, such as hot springs, waterfalls, lakes and reservoirs, and major parks.

Finding the site: This is where roughly half the value of this book lies—detailed directions right to a spot. Some of these directions are tricky—if you were to look at a map where "X marks the spot," you might not be able to tell which direction to come in from. Each site listed here contains road names and numbers, but some are on trails or long-unused roads. In most cases I started from a significant landmark or major highway. In those few instances where the mileage I wrote down seemed off, I went with Google Earth information, but I don't always trust their data either. In rare but documented cases, Google Earth will take you across bridges that don't exist, such as the nonexistent entry from the east to Leonia Knob, or on roads that haven't been built. So I took it and Google Maps and MapQuest and all the online resources with a grain of salt. I know not everyone has a GPS unit, but if you don't, you should. I also noted wherever I believe I came in from the wrong way. All locales were field-checked again by 2019, but we all know that things change.

Rockhounding: In the final section of each site write-up, I covered the basic information you need for success. I tried to resist the tendency to supply only a terse paragraph of general information, while also fighting the urge to go into way more depth than necessary for most readers. If there was good geology involved, I brought it up. Some of these locales are self-evident if you can just get to them. The truth is that with a strong vehicle and a dedicated copilot, you could cross off just about every site in this book with one epic summer road trip. Getting there with good directions is way more than half the battle. Some sites will relinquish their prizes within 30 minutes, and there isn't much to do except drive on. Other locales could serve as a base camp for a weeklong operation, and you leave feeling like you've barely scratched the surface. In each case, I described the fastest and/or surest path to success and supplied enough background to get you started.

If you find something in the "Rockhounding" description you'd like to concentrate on and want to learn more about, here are some suggestions: Crystal collector? Want more of the science behind gem specimens? Get Lanny Ream's books and dig in. Want more fossils? If you want more historic sites to explore, get Tim Fisher's *Ore-Rock-On* DVD. Love gold prospecting? I've got a few sites here, and the companion book *Gold Panning the Pacific Northwest* (FalconGuides) will keep you busy. Love the science of geology? For more pure science, visit the Idaho Geological Survey website and pick up the *Roadside Geology* book for Idaho. Looking for coins and nuggets? Metal detector hobbyists can try the Wells and Sparling ghost town books. See appendix A and the bibliography for details on these and other resources.

1. Priest Lake

See map on page 20.

Land type: Lakeshore, forested creek bank
County: Bonner
GPS: A: 48.62998, -116.88338; 2,443 feet (Priest Lake)
    B: 48.82120, -116.97632; 2,978 feet (Gold Creek)
Best season: Summer; low water exposes better gravels.
Land manager: USDA Forest Service–Kaniksu National Forest
Material: Gold, quartz crystals, feldspar crystals; tumbler material
Tools: Geology pick, gold-panning equipment
Vehicle: Anything sturdy; an ATV would be nice on Quartz Crystals Road.
Accommodations: Developed camping at Roosevelt Cedars Grove and around the lakes; Dickensheet Campground is easy to get to, right on the Priest River. Abundant primitive camping on nearby national forest lands; resorts near Nordman.
Special attractions: Panhandle Historic Rivers Passage Scenic Byway. Upper Priest Lake is a hidden gem, and maps show low-grade copper mines around the northwestern shore.

Scenic Priest Lake offers excellent tumbler material at many of its beaches.

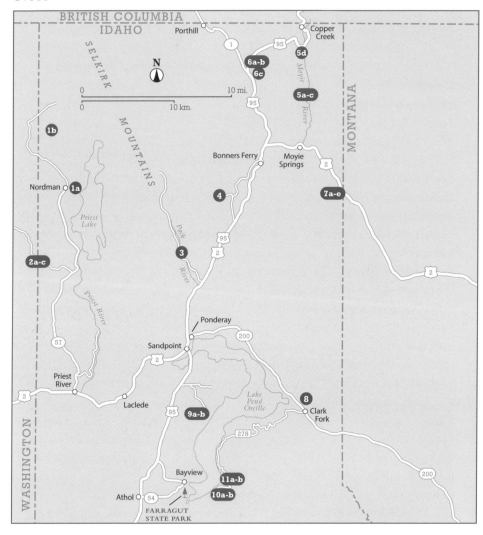

Finding the site: From US 2 at the town of Priest River, swing north on ID 57 to Nordman. Site A is on Priest Lake at the Ledgewood Picnic Area. From Nordman, take Reeder Bay Road/NFD 1339 east about 3 miles until you see the sign.

Site B is entirely optional, but it's a nice tour. Drive north on ID 57; it takes on many names: West Side Road, Nordman Road, and finally NF 302. About 12.5 miles from Nordman, note the Stagger Inn Campground; payment is on the honor system. Technically, this excellent campground is in Washington, but it's a good setup route for this part of Idaho's Panhandle. The hike around the nearby falls is quite good, but a little slick. Note that this is bear country. At 1.7 miles from the campground, you'll see a sign for Quartz Crystals Road, which is gated. I'm told there are good crystals "somewhere" on this road, hence the name, but we didn't find them, so I didn't list it. It would help if the road wasn't gated. About 4.7 miles past the junction with Quartz Crystals Road, there is a small set of tracks off to the left, leading down to the creek. Look for additional access to the creek if this spot is taken.

Rockhounding

There are many pegmatites in the granites to the west of Priest Lake, especially farther east in Washington. Pegmatites are coarse crystalline granite or other igneous rock sometimes with interesting quartz crystals several centimeters to several meters in length. The beach at Site A primarily contains remnants of the local batholith, with small polished pebbles of granite, quartz, feldspar, jasper, and related material. Take your time and fill a sample

Search for quartzite and jasper among the granite and pebbles wherever you can find gravel concentrations.

bag. The gravel is on the small side, but the amount of polish makes up for the size. The swimming here is outstanding as well. Priest River drains the lake to the south via Outlet Bay, and there is access to river rock via primitive roads for several miles after clearing the lake. Dickensheet Campground has good camping right on the river, with a good selection of gravels.

The gold at Site B is very fine. We found a nice inside bend and panned out some colors, and the gravels here were full of decomposed Kaniksu Batholith, mostly granite, but with rounded feldspar crystals and enough clear broken quartz to make things interesting. Most of this area did not have enough mineralization to make for extensive hard-rock mining. You can see from old topo maps that there was some mining activity above Upper Priest Lake, but not much came of it. There aren't even roads to the upper lake; it will require a hike or boat from the main lake. The big Continental Mine, closer to the Canadian border, is an active claim, but there are some small silver, lead, gold, copper, and zinc prospects to the east, south of the top of Grass Mountain.

2. Solo Creek

See map on page 20.

Land type: Forested hillside

County: Pend Oreille, Washington

GPS: A: 48.47659, -117.05909; 2,755 feet (parking)

B: 48.47649, -117.05756; 2,750 feet (camping)

C: 48.47559, -117.05913; 2,758 feet (diggings)

Best season: Spring through fall

Land manager: USDA Forest Service–Colville National Forest

Material: Quartz crystals, smoky quartz

Tools: Shovel, screen, geology pick; bring water.

Vehicle: Any

Accommodations: Primitive camping along the creek at Site B; abundant primitive camping on nearby national forest lands to the west; developed camping around Priest Lake

Special attractions: Panhandle Historic Rivers Passage Scenic Byway; Priest Lake

Finding the site: From the town of Priest River on US 2, go north on ID 57. Drive 21.5 miles, almost to Dickensheet Junction, and take a left on Squaw Valley Loop.

The camping area at Site B offers good trails to the diggings.

After 0.3 mile, this road connects to NFD 312. Head west on NFD 312 for 7 miles, whereupon you have actually crossed into Washington. At the T junction, turn left on NFD 659 and drive 0.7 mile. There is a wide spot for parking, and the diggings are up the hill on the left. This road continues west, and will eventually take you into Usk along WA 20.

Rockhounding

The quartz crystals here run big and rough, usually not found as perfect crystals. The quartz tends to be well-terminated with clean faces. I have found fragments within minutes of hopping out of the car, and at one point when we pulled in very, very late, I even found shattered crystals by flashlight. So even though the locale is 0.7 mile from the Idaho state line, I included it here.

My best advice is to hike around the diggings and get a feel for the spot. The trail loops from the camping area, up and over, and then leads to the road again. Find a recent pit with good-looking fragments around it and start widening the spot. Use a shovel and a screen and bring a little spray bottle to wash off material. Use patience so that you don't smash a good crystal, and be careful rooting around with bare fingers, as the crystal edges can draw blood.

The material comes from a pegmatite and is better at depth. However, do not tunnel here, and do not cause any rocks to clutter up the road. Be sure to pick up some trash while you're here too; previous diggers have left some messes.

There are additional areas nearby in Washington where pegmatites have given up mica and beryl. Refer to the bibliography.

Log trucks use NFD 659, so don't leave gear or tools in the road when you work up above. The area feels very remote until you hear a big diesel engine groaning down the hill under a load.

It takes a lot of digging to get crystals with good terminations and clean crystal faces.

3. Pack River

See map on page 20.
Land type: Riverbanks, road cut
County: Boundary
GPS: 48.51628, -116.58056; 2,310 feet (Pack River)
Best season: Late spring through summer
Land manager: USDA Forest Service–Kaniksu National Forest
Material: Tiny garnets; tumbler material such as quartzite, granite, and feldspar
Tools: Geology pick, screen, gold pan
Vehicle: Any; 4WD suggested for gravel roads

Gravels along the Pack River contain mostly granite. Search the smaller material for quartzite, jasper, and feldspar; plus, pan for garnet and black sands.

Accommodations: Lots of primitive camping spots on nearby national forest lands; developed camping at Roman Nose Lakes

Special attractions: Wild Horse Trail Scenic Byway; Roman Nose Lakes; Ruby Pass

Finding the site: From US 95/US 2 at the gas station near Samuels, go northwest on NFD 231/Upper Pack River Road. Drive about 8 miles to the OHV (off-highway vehicle) park. About 0.15 mile past the big parking area, look for a road diving back down to the right to the riverbank. This is the site. It won't look like it during high water, but this is a ford. We just parked here and explored.

Rockhounding

The Pack River contains a good mix of material from the Kaniksu Batholith, including granite, quartz, feldspar, garnet, and mica. This site is a pleasant, shady spot to pull over and wade around, even when the water is in full run-off mode. You might even get to watch someone try to ford the river here, so park carefully. Try panning for garnets; you should get plenty of small purple crystals. If the main spot is occupied, try 48.52362, -116.58818.

There are more river access points all the way up, and some good road cuts to check out for mica and feldspar. The road crosses the river at about 13 miles from the highway, with more exposures to search. The prizes here are feldspar and quartz crystals, but they're hard to find in matrix. There's a good granite quarry at 48.57450, -116.61261 near the last bridge.

Another search area is along Caribou Creek. We pecked at a few outcrops up here when researching the first edition and found mica flakes large enough to spot from the car. Most of those are gone, but some exploring might yield more.

4. Ruby Creek

See map on page 20.
Land type: Creek bank
County: Boundary
GPS: 48.63143, -116.46778; 3,159 feet
Best season: Late spring through fall
Land manager: USDA Forest Service–Kaniksu National Forest
Material: Tumbler material, garnet
Tools: Geology pick, shovel, screen, gold pan
Vehicle: Any, but 4WD suggested (gravel roads)

Garnet is easy to pan near the bridge across Ruby Creek, but the crystals are small.

Accommodations: Lots of primitive camping spots on nearby national forest lands; large pull-out about 0.1 mile farther up the road; developed camping at Roman Nose Lakes

Special attractions: Wild Horse Trail Scenic Byway; Roman Nose Lakes; Ruby Pass

Finding the site: From US 2 at Naples, turn west on Schoolhouse Road. Trail Creek Road leads east at this intersection. Drive 0.1 mile west on Schoolhouse Road to Old US 95; turn right to head north. Drive 0.7 mile, then turn left onto Highland Flats Road. Stay on Highland Flats for 2.3 miles, then turn right onto Ruby Creek Road. Drive 4.1 miles to the bridge across Ruby Creek. There is a bit of a trick to reach the creek; the improved logging road will try to lure you into staying on it about 0.2 mile before the bridge. Be extremely cautious of logging trucks as you near the coordinates; there were several active operations here, and plenty more trees to cut in the future.

Rockhounding

Ruby Creek is another misnamed geographic feature; the old-timers were hoping they'd found a creek full of rubies, but instead the small, bright-red crystals are almandine garnet. This creek has plenty of small, well-formed deep-red to purple crystals, with occasional larger specimens. The smaller crystals are usually complete, but larger ones will often show fractures. Again, this small creek contains a good mix of material from the Kaniksu Batholith, including granite, quartz, feldspar, garnet, and mica. This site is easy to access, especially above the bridge, as there is an easy trail down.

Tiny garnets from several pans

This road gets increasingly worse as you near the top at Ruby Pass, but the views are spectacular.

5. Moyie River

See map on page 20.
Land type: Forested riverbank
County: Boundary
GPS: A: 48.81969, -116.14652; 2,309 feet (Meadow Creek Campground)
    B: 48.83782, -116.13852; 2,826 feet (Placer Creek)
    C: 48.82495, -116.16574; 2,397 feet (bridge)
    D: 48.91993, -116.17922; 2,550 feet (Moyie Crossing)
Best season: Summer; low water required
Land manager: USDA Forest Service–Kaniksu National Forest
Material: Fine gold, small flakes, black sands; garnets
Tools: Gold pan, shovel, screens
Vehicle: 4WD suggested; required if driving in from south
Accommodations: Developed camping at Copper Creek and Meadow Creek campgrounds; plenty of primitive camping sites on national forest lands

Moyie Falls during high water. Later in the year, pan the gravels above here toward Addie for gold, garnets, and black sands.

Special attractions: Moyie Falls for spring runoff; Copper Falls, out of Addie

Finding the site: Most folks will start from Moyie Falls, but do not try to take the road that closely follows the Moyie River north of town; this road is extremely rough in places. Instead take Meadow Creek Road, about 2 miles east of US 95, or 3.5 miles west of Moyie Falls. After 0.3 mile the road takes a hard right to stay on Meadow Creek Road then continues for 10.1 miles to intersect Moyie River Road. This is a key intersection; take the right, go just 0.3 mile, then turn left to the Meadow Creek Campground. To reach Placer Creek, go back to that junction, stay right, cross the bridge in 0.3 mile, and stay right to begin on CR 34-1/Deer Ridge Road. Follow this road for 2.1 miles to where it bears sharply to the right; there is a spur that leads to the left, with a gate before the bridge over Placer Creek. To reach the "bridge" site, go back to Moyie River Road but do not go south, back across the bridge. Instead, start north. You will see a faint dirt track that leads to the water and a decent camping spot. Finally, to reach Moyie Crossing, resume north on Moyie River Road for 7.7 miles and look for a left turn across the railroad tracks. If you are here during the right season, the gate will be open and you can drive in; we had to walk, but it was a short jaunt.

Rockhounding

Use screens to make nice, rich samples and then pan down to concentrates. The Moyie River isn't noted for big flakes and nuggets, but there is ample black sand and flour gold. The trick is to screen down a lot of river sand while digging around big rocks and natural riffles. The best time of year is when the water is low; if you can access any of the numerous small islands, search the front end, where the water begins to slow down. We saw numerous black streaks along the riverbank where the water velocity slowed enough to start dumping heavy material. Anywhere south from this easy-access spot will offer good opportunities to get a sample.

This area of the Panhandle region is full of mineralization, although much of it seems to be zinc, copper, and base metals. The Moyie River gives up good color, however, and the area around Placer Creek is by far the best. If you look on maps, the source of the area's garnets is obvious—Ruby Mountain and Ruby Ridge dominate the skyline to the east. Placer Creek has good color, and it empties into the Moyie River right across from Meadow Creek Campground. The upper Placer Creek site listed will also work if it is too crowded in the campground, and the road connects yet again with Placer Creek even higher up. I liked the Bridge locale (Site C) listed here, as you

Decomposing quartz vein along the Moyie River

can combine placering with a little lode sampling. There is a nice quartz seam exposed on the north side of the bedrock outcrop, and it has the characteristic rusty staining you like to see from decomposing sulfides. You can even try crushing up a sample and panning it. The Moyie River Crossing does not have great gold, but it contains some historic significance as a washed-out bridge. It also features an interesting outdoor sculpture by Jeffrey Funk titled Kaniksu Passage. He balanced large slabs of angular argillite on rounded granite and surrounded it with giant salmon circling patiently. It is a nice picnic area for the kids to blow off some steam. Copper Falls, at the top of the Moyie River Road and then back up NFD 2517, is well marked and worth a hike.

Other rockhounding opportunities in this area include the road above Copper Falls, which crosses a few low-quality copper outcrops. This whole area just didn't have enough good mineralization to get heavily mined. If you have a stout vehicle, you can visit Copper Ridge and Ruby Ridge and at least collect an interesting sample that few other rockhounds can match. Note that the nearby Buckhorn Mine is about an 8-mile round-trip hike unless your ATV can get up there.

6. Tungsten Hill

See map on page 20.

Land type: Mine tailings in mountain forest

County: Boundary

GPS: A: 48.92263, -116.33449; 3,131 feet (jeep trail)
    B: 48.91875, -116.33142; 3,310 feet (ruins)
    C: 48.89360, -116.30421; 3,583 feet (Bethlehem Mine)

Best season: Summer through fall

Land manager: USDA Forest Service–Kaniksu National Forest

Material: Gold, silver, lead, zinc, molybdenum

Tools: Heavy hammer

Vehicle: 4WD suggested

Accommodations: Primitive camping throughout the area on national forest lands; developed camping at Brush Lake

Special attractions: Wild Horse Trail Scenic Byway; Canadian boundary at Porthill and Eastport

Finding the site: From "downtown" Bonners Ferry just south of the bridge, drive 16.9 miles north on US 95. Turn right (south) onto Brush Lake Road. At 0.3 mile, turn left onto FR 5591, and drive 2.3 miles until you see a faint jeep trail coming in

The cabin at Site B is near the American Girl adit and tailings. Search for sulfide ores such as malachite in quartz veins here; also look for scheelite, the ore of tungsten.

from the right. Hike about 0.4 mile up the hill, following the bumpy road until you see the old cabin. This is Site B for reference; continue on to the T in the road, and stay right. You'll see a large tailings pile on the right, with the actual mine entrance on the left above it. To reach Site C, hike back to the vehicle, backtrack 2.3 miles to the turn, and drive left onto Camp 9 Road/Bethlehem Mine Road. Drive about 3 miles, then note the turn to the left. After 0.2 mile you'll see the gate to the right. Park here and walk another 0.1 mile. You'll see a tailings dump of specimens to pick through; a little farther, you'll see the old foundations. (The cabin has been torn down since the first edition was published.) Up the hill from there are the vent shafts to the underground workings, which are gated for safety.

Rockhounding

Look for quartz with rusty staining on the mine dumps and rock piles throughout this area, and also along the roads. Bring a heavy hammer and break up the larger rocks to get to fresh material inside. Scheelite, the ore for tungsten, is not a particularly striking specimen, but you should be able to detect small black crystals if you break up enough rock. The silver ore is black or dull gray, and harder to find. I didn't notice any galena crystals, and the gold is bound up at a micro level and even harder to discern. Bring a hand lens to see what's going on, or settle for specimens with the green ore for copper: malachite. The American Girl Mine at Site B contained silver, lead, copper, molybdenum, gold, and zinc; the Bethlehem Mine produced copper, zinc, gold, silver, and tungsten. The shaft for the Bethlehem Mine is at 48.89354, –116.30444. Note that the American Girl underground claim is for sale, so restrict your surface collecting to a specimen or two from the dumps.

Malachite is by far the easiest specimen to locate at Tungsten Hill.

Farther up around the loop, you can also find the Tungsten Hill Mine, Regal Mine, and Queen Mine among others, with more of the same material. Check a topo map for exact locales. North on ID 1 toward Canada is the Golden Scepter Mine, but it has been under claim and may be active again.

Hungry mosquitoes are thick up here; bring bug spray.

7. Leonia Knob

See map on page 20.

Land type: Ghost town in mountain forest
County: Boundary
GPS: A: 48.62473, -116.06736; 2,557 feet (trailhead)
    B: 48.61477, -116.07752; 2,769 feet (prospect)
    C: 48.59908, -116.09299; 2,592 feet (road)
    D: 48.59751, -116.09279; 2,564 feet (bridge)
    E: 48.60327, -116.08397; 2,594 feet (ruins)
Best season: Summer through fall
Land manager: USDA Forest Service–Kaniksu National Forest
Material: Gold and associated mineralization, such as pyrite
Tools: Heavy hammer, chisels
Vehicle: Any
Accommodations: Primitive camping on national forest lands throughout the area
Special attractions: Wild Horse Trail Scenic Byway; old ghost town of Boulder City (not much left)
Finding the site: Drive to the north end of Bonners Ferry on Main Street/US 95/ US 2, but before the big bridge, turn right (east) onto Ash Street. Follow Ash for 0.3 mile; turn left onto Cow Creek Road/CR 24 and follow it for 2.6 miles. Stay left onto Crossport Road/CR24 for 2.9 miles, then turn left onto Katka Road. Stay on Katka for 3.8 miles, then stay right to remain on CR 24. Drive 8.1 miles to the trailhead sign; you are now on USFS land. To reach Site B, continue 1 mile and look for safe parking; the prospects are down the hill. To reach Site C, continue 1.3 miles, then stay left to continue on Twentymile Leonia Road for 0.8 mile. You should spot a road off to the right, which will parallel Boulder Creek but stay far above it. There is primitive camping in here. Site D is just 0.1 mile farther on the main road, where you'll find the bridge and easy access to the creek. Continue on the main road 0.5 mile; stay left, and in another 500 feet there is a turn to the left to parking and some rotting timbers.

My GPS kept suggesting that I drive into Montana and take a bridge across the river to get to Leonia Knob, so on one trip I finally checked it out. Bad idea; the bridge is long gone. Don't make that mistake; use this route instead.

Rockhounding

The nearby Homestake Mine, reached via NFD 2612 after driving about 7.6 miles on CR 24, is roughly at 48.63486, -116.07154, but it's on patented land and off-limits to collectors without prior permission. There is some quartz on the road here, but most of it has been scooped up.

Site A is the trailhead that leads down to the creek mouth where it enters the Kootenay River. I used it for reference only; the hike is interesting if you want to pan down there. Site B is close to a major prospect, which you'll have to bushwhack a bit to locate down the hill. There are two main areas of open, white ground. The GPS coordinates are directly up the hill of the east patch, so you'll want to wind over to the right eventually to reach the second. Search for gold and silver ore, with galena and sphalerite accessories. There is plentiful float to pick up and inspect all over the area, and you should be able to get a decent sample of sulfides from this historic site. Be prepared to break up white quartz to get to fresh areas free of oxidation, and bring a hand lens. We hiked the "road" that leads down all the way to Boulder Creek, and it wasn't too hard to negotiate—until the hike back up.

Boulder Creek shows plenty of bedrock at Site D, where you can pan for gold and garnets and search the gravels for quartz with rusty staining.

Silvery pyrite cubes found in a hand specimen from Boulder Creek

Site C is the beginning of the jeep trail that leads along Boulder Creek. We drove in a good distance to some primitive camping areas. Supposedly there was a trail for about a mile to the mining areas, but it dead-ended after about 0.5 mile. Site D has excellent creek access and camping on both sides of the bridge, and you can pan here for color or check for garnets. Site E is more ruins that were part of the Idamont Mine and the old ghost town of Boulder City; the ruins continue across the road and aren't too hard to find.

According to news accounts, around 1910 mining promoter J. M. Schnatterly founded Boulder City, also known as Ruby City, in an extravagant swindle. There were tales of fist-size rubies from this area, but geologists never verified a source, and they were probably large garnets. Schnatterly claimed to have located a 15-inch-wide vein of radium ore to promote his venture, but long after the fact, there are doubts the ore ever existed; again, the geology just doesn't match up. Nevertheless, the Idaho Gold and Ruby Mining Company raised $2 million and set up a large sluice (and an aerial tram), the largest in the world at the time. But after washing tons of gravel, barely $150 worth of gold came from the effort. When the gold and rubies failed to materialize, efforts slowed down tremendously. Schnatterly died in an explosion on his boat on the Kootenay River in 1923; the property limped along until the 1930s then folded.

8. Clark Fork

See map on page 20.
Land type: Forested road cut, open streambed
County: Bonner
GPS: 48.15076, -116.15902; 2,140 feet (road cut)
Best season: Summer through fall
Land manager: USDA Forest Service–Kaniksu National Forest
Material: Fossil stromatolites, aventurine; tumbler material
Tools: Geology pick; heavy hammer helpful
Vehicle: Any; sites very close to main highway
Accommodations: Developed camping at Porcupine Lake; primitive camping on national forest lands to the north and also along the Clark Fork near the Montana border
Special attractions: Pend Oreille Scenic Byway; Cabinet Gorge Dam
Finding the site: From Clark Fork on ID 200, head northeast on Main Street for 0.4 mile. Swing right with the road as it becomes NFD 276/Mosquito Creek Road. Avoid the turn for NFD 419/Lightning Creek Road, which swings to the left about 0.6 mile from the highway. About 0.5 mile farther up NFD 276, or about 1.1 miles from the highway, you should see a large road cut on the left. This site contains rusty fossil stromatolites and green aventurine.

Rockhounding

Roadside Geology of Idaho (see bibliography) suggests there are fossil stromatolites in the road cuts along the road to Cabinet, but we only found a little calcite and some interesting psilomelane—a manganese mineral noted for its fractal dendrites, which look like little fossil branches. Also, most of the road cuts were dangerous to stop at. We kept children firmly belted in the back seat for those stops. On a whim, we tried a back road, and that's where we found easier access.

The fossil stromatolites, which I believe are part of the Paleozoic Libby Formation, are wavy, rusty folds in the rock. Don't be fooled—they may be ugly, but they represent the biggest jump in life on Earth since single-cell blue-green algae developed. Stromatolites are colonies of algae that have learned to live together, and they were the most advanced life on the planet for some time.

This road cut contains interesting fossil stromatolites, which display a distinctive wavy banding. Also look for green aventurine.

This stromatolite specimen is rusting away, but where still hard, this rock will take a nice polish.

The green aventurine is a common yard rock in many western gardens, as landscaping shops carry it in various sizes. Aventurine is a variety of translucent quartzite with small plates of fuchsite, a green chrome-rich mica. The sparkly appearance is known as "aventurescence." Aventurine is usually green, but there are also yellow, red, pink, brown, white, gray, and blue varieties.

The literature suggests that several mines near Clark Fork contain native copper and copper minerals such as azurite, chalcocite, chalcopyrite, cuprite, and malachite. Unfortunately, the Hope Mine and Lawrence Mine are gated and posted, and the Hope Mine may have also been wiped away by flooding. Other mines in the area hosted zinc, copper, silver, and lead. You might be able to spot some interesting mineralization in road cuts or along fresh logging roads.

This gorge saw repeated inundations from the Missoula Floods during the Pleistocene; glacial lobes dammed the Clark Fork and fell apart, releasing millions of gallons of water that carved across southeast Washington and inundated the Willamette River Valley far away. Look for evidence of enormous ripple marks above the current river. In 1910 at the University of Washington, J. Harlen Bretz began developing his then-ridiculed theory that there had been repeated catastrophic flooding about 15,000 years ago. It took several decades before his theories were generally accepted. Check the Ice Age Floods Institute online (iafi.org) for more information.

9. Talache

See map on page 20.

Land type: Tailings and scattered debris in forested mountain area

County: Bonner

GPS: A: 48.15359, -116.50635; 3,182 feet (Silver Butte adit)
B: 48.16079, -116.51242; 3,433 feet (quartz ridge)

Best season: Spring through fall

Land manager: Idaho Department of State Lands

Material: Quartz float containing malachite and galena

Tools: Geology pick

Vehicle: 4WD if gate is open; any if parked at gate. An ATV would be nice.

Accommodations: None at site; developed camping on Lake Pend Oreille at Garfield Bay and Green Bay

Special attractions: Panhandle Historic Rivers Passage Scenic Byway; Wild Horse Trail Scenic Byway; Pend Oreille Scenic Byway; Lake Pend Oreille, Bottle Bay, Talache Landing

Finding the site: About 5.3 miles south of Sandpoint on US 95, turn left (east) onto Sagle Road. After 1.3 miles turn right (south) onto Talache Road. After about 3.6 miles turn right onto unmarked Moyles Road. Park at the gate if it is locked (don't block it!) and walk up the steep road; you may have to dodge a few ATVs. If

This is the adit for the Silver Butte Mine, Site A. Look for quartz with rusty staining, and break it open to find ore for gold, zinc, silver, lead, and antimony. Stay out of the mine!

the gate is open, figure that it could close by the end of the day, so time your visit. About 0.5 mile past the gate, you'll reach an intersection of sorts; the main road continues right. Go about 0.3 mile and take a left, down the hill. Site A is about 0.3 mile on this rough road. To reach Site B, backtrack to the main road 0.3 mile, then take a left and go about 0.6 mile. The main road goes left, but stay right and go up the steep hill. The mineralization is about 0.2 mile up this road; this is Site B.

Rockhounding

The quartz in this area contains gold, sphalerite, silver, galena, and stibnite, so look for anything metallic in veins. Site A has good material scattered throughout the road, so don't bother with the adit. The road is steep to the Silver Butte, but a sturdy 4WD vehicle can make it. We walked. This area is near Bimetallic Ridge and shows good mineralization throughout. Site B is an area with extensive quartz outcrops and plenty of mineralization. There are other mines in the area, so there is more potential for exploration.

After clearing the gate, the road makes a sharp right turn, with a decent road going off a short distance to the left. There are two adits near the end of this left-hand road and some good rock piles. The main road keeps going past my GPS reading, and a jeep trail off to the right has at least four prospects and adits along its route. A little farther up, another jeep trail turns off to the left, with an adit basically at the first corner. Even farther, the road Ts and there are minor prospects to the left. To the right is the trail to the main Hope and Faith Shaft, less than 0.25 mile away.

Start your search at Talache by identifying green malachite, then work your way to fresh metallic ores for lead (galena) and zinc (sphalerite).

Nearby areas proved disappointing. The main Talache Mine, closer to the lake, is under development by the Shoshone Silver Mining Company. We looked around the railroad tracks 2 miles south of Sagle for the feldspar crystals mentioned by Ream (see bibliography), but the best thing we found there was a big red-eared pond turtle. We drove over to Bottle Bay and found pink granite.

10. Chloride Gulch

See map on page 20.

Land type: Forested creek bed
County: Bonner
GPS: A: 47.93709, -116.44899; 2,629 feet (Chloride Gulch)
    B: 47.93527, -116.44584; 2,665 feet (cabin)
Best season: Late summer through early fall
Land manager: USDA Forest Service–Kaniksu National Forest
Material: Black sands and fine gold, plus quartz containing ores of silver, lead, and zinc, such as galena and sphalerite

Search for fossil-bearing limestone and ore-bearing quartz boulders at Chloride Gulch.

Tools: Gold pan, shovel, screens, heavy hammer

Vehicle: 4WD strongly suggested; rough road in places to Lakeview

Accommodations: Scattered campsites along the lake; abundant primitive camping on extensive national forest lands; some rustic resorts in the area

Special attractions: Farragut State Park; Panhandle Historic Rivers Passage Scenic Byway; Wild Horse Trail Scenic Byway; Pend Oreille Scenic Byway; nice overlook of southern Lake Pend Oreille

Finding the site: From the Athol exit on US 95, exit east on ID 54. Drive 6 miles; at the traffic circle turn right onto North Good Hope Road. Drive 2 miles, then turn left onto East Bunco Road/NFD 209. Drive 7.8 miles, and then turn left onto NFD 332. (Note: Your GPS may suggest Lakeview Cutoff Road, but in 2019 it was a nasty, narrow road with underbrush that scraped both sides of the vehicle.) After 0.3 mile turn left and drive another 6.3 miles on NFD 332. Turn right onto Lakeview Road and follow it for 1.1 miles to the coordinates at the gulch; this is Site A. The old cabin at Site B is 0.5 mile farther on Lakeview Road. In another 0.1 mile there is a right turn to the Lakeview Mine, which may be in production now and is fenced off.

Rockhounding

The water dries up by late June, so be forewarned that you may not be able to pan here. We were lucky to have enough water to work in the bottom of the gulch, but you may have to fill a bucket and work it somewhere else. If you

The rocks at Chloride Gulch are clean and easy to break up with a hammer.

can get a nice concentrate sample, check it with a hand lens or microscope for flour gold. Concentrates from Chloride Gulch should also be rich in silver, lead, and zinc.

The gulch has plenty of material to pick over, and it is easy to access. Later, we were glad we stopped here, as most of the mines in this area are now under active claim of the Shoshone Silver Mining Company, which restarted its Lakeview mill in September 2007. Their stock price was about 18 cents a share in late 2009, but it has since been delisted. There was little activity there in summer 2019.

Walk up and down the gulch and use a heavy hammer to break up interesting rocks. The mines in the Lakeview District exploit Precambrian Belt Series rocks known for lead and silver. These are the same rocks associated with the massive silver deposits farther south in the Coeur d'Alene Mining District's famed Silver Valley, but not as rich. Look for rusty staining on nice quartz samples, and see if you can detect a little galena or silvery ore as you break up the rock to find fresh material. Most of the ore here is a sulfide of one form or another and oxidizes quickly upon contact with the air or water. Like many lead-silver deposits, this ore isn't the prettiest of specimens, but if you can get fresh material, it looks better.

The limestones in the Lakeview area are said to contain trilobite fragments. We found only coral fossil fragments, so more research is needed, but check as many outcrops as you dare.

11. Vulcan Mine

See map on page 20.

Land type: Road cut and tailings pile in forested hillside

County: Bonner

GPS: A: 47.97850, -116.42927; 3,138 feet (road cut on NFD 278)

     B: 47.98052, -116.43301; 3,204 feet (Vulcan Mine)

Best season: Summer through early fall

Land manager: USDA Forest Service–Kaniksu National Forest

Material: Skarn deposit minerals, such as pyrite and quartz

Tools: Heavy hammer, geology pick; gold pan to sample creeks

Vehicle: 4WD required

Accommodations: Developed camping along the lake; primitive camping throughout the area on national forest lands

Special attractions: Panhandle Historic Rivers Passage Scenic Byway; Pend Oreille Scenic Byway. NFD 278 takes you all the way around the southern end of the lake,

The boat dock at Lakeview has an outhouse and a short beach with tumbler material, plus a great view of Lake Pend Oreille.

Tailings at the Vulcan Mine are rusty with oxidized pyrite. Bring a heavy hammer to break up larger rocks and reach fresh material.

past the Minerva Mine, Shafer Peak, and a big lime quarry. There are reports of fossil trilobites in the limestones south of the lake.

Finding the site: From the Athol exit on US 95, exit east on ID 54. Drive 6 miles; at the traffic circle, turn right onto North Good Hope Road. Drive 2 miles, then turn left onto East Bunco Road/NFD 209. Drive 7.8 miles, and turn left onto NFD 332. (Note: Your GPS may suggest Lakeview Cutoff Road, but in 2019 it was a nasty, narrow road with underbrush that scraped both sides of the vehicle.) After 0.3 mile turn left and drive another 6.3 miles on NFD 332; turn right onto Lakeview Road. Drive 2.3 miles, and then either take Main Street another 1.1 miles to the dock at the lake or skip it and turn left onto NFD 278. Drive 4.6 miles to the road cut, which is Site A. (Alternatively, you could drive past the dock in Lakeview and follow a very rough road straight to the coordinates for the Vulcan Mine, about 3.3 miles from the dock.) To reach Site B, continue about 0.5 mile to the transmission lines; hike down the hill about 0.3 mile.

About 0.5 mile farther on NFD 278 from Site A, look very closely for a faint 4WD track leading down the hill to the left. We parked here and walked, but if you are brave and have a strong rig, you can drive. The Vulcan Mine is about 0.4 mile down this road/trail; look for the apron of rusty orange dirt piled up above the road within the transmission line right-of-way. This is Site B.

Rockhounding

At Site A, try to bust up some of the large boulders to get to the fresh pyrite within. Do not leave any rocks in the road, and if you spy any trash, grab it while you're there. (In most jurisdictions, the USFS will ticket folks who make a big mess at a road cut.) You shouldn't have to do any digging here to get fresh rocks to break open.

At Site B, the Vulcan Mine, try to find more pyrite material. We searched in vain for the main adit here, but it was either hidden or caved in, as we didn't find it. It's probably just as well, as the fumes can build up to dangerous levels. We found plenty of rocks to break up, and we left with some good pyrite stringers. The smell here is heavy with sulfur, as this is a skarn deposit and noted for sulfides such as pyrite. A skarn is a metamorphic zone developed in the contact area around igneous rock intrusions when carbonate sedimentary rocks are invaded. The mineralization can be impressive.

Look for tiny vugs such as this one at the Vulcan Mine, with tiny pyrite crystals peeking out.

12. Pine Creek

See map on page 48.

Land type: Large creek valley

County: Shoshone

GPS: A: 47.48371, -116.23179; 2,431 feet (pull-off)

  B: 47.47075, -116.20734; 2,591 feet (Hilarity Mine)

  C: 47.46581, -116.19725; 2,616 feet (Highland Creek)

Best season: Summer through fall

Land manager: BLM–Coeur d'Alene

Material: Black sands, silver/lead ore in quartz

Tools: Gold pan, geology pick

Vehicle: Any; 4WD required for exploring

Accommodations: Developed camping on Coeur d'Alene Lake and north of Prichard, along the Coeur d'Alene River

Special attractions: Lake Coeur d'Alene Scenic Byway. Wallace is a great family-friendly town with museums and mine tours.

The Silver Valley contains numerous old mining structures to photograph. Do not trespass or enter any buildings.

Sites 12–16

Finding the site: From I-90 get off at exit 45 for Pinehurst and turn right from the ramp. Drive south 1.4 miles then turn right onto Division. Continue 1.4 miles and stay on the main route; it is now named Pine Creek Road. Drive another 2.6 miles and park safely on the right. To reach Site B, drive another 1.6 miles and park to the left. Site C is another 0.6 mile up the road to the mouth of Highland Creek.

Rockhounding

The Pine Creek Mining District is actually part of the world-famous Coeur d'Alene Mining District, known as "Silver Valley." This western end of the largest silver-producing district in the world offers several opportunities to view the remains of old flotation mills, some mine dumps, and extensive gravel bars for easy rockhounding and panning elusive gold colors.

Massive gray galena with yellow gold, from one of the Silver Valley mines

Site A, the first good pull-off I found, offers the chance to pan a little concentrate and with luck collect some metal ore associated with quartz. This isn't great tumbler material, per se—the old Precambrian Belt Series rocks just don't provide collectors with much agate or jasper. But you should be able to find heavily mineralized quartz that proves you were in the area. Try breaking the white rocks up—some might be calcite, but most are quartz. Look for rusty staining, black streaks and veinlets, and pay particular attention to any rocks that seem unduly heavy.

The old Liberal King Mill was torn down after the first edition reached print, but there are still a few old structures up here worth hunting with your camera. Imagine this tiny valley teeming with miners, working at least ten different mines. Zinc, silver, lead, gold, and copper all emerged from the underground mines here.

If you have the right vehicle, try to get onto the steep mountain roads to the east as you get farther up the East Fork of Pine Creek. On a good day you can take Burma Road up into the hills. At Site C you can look for outcrops along Highland Road, dip a pan in the East Fork of Pine Creek, or venture up Highland Creek Road to the ruins at 47.48453, -116.17789.

13. Crystal Gold Mine

See map on page 48.

Land type: Underground mine
County: Shoshone
GPS: 47.53225, -116.09224; 2,348 feet (51931 Silver Valley Rd., Kellogg)
Best season: Year-round. Check goldmine-idaho.com for seasonal hours; closed on major holidays.
Land manager: Private
Material: Mine tour
Tools: Camera
Vehicle: Any
Accommodations: Motels all along the interstate freeway; developed camping on Coeur d'Alene Lake and north of Prichard, along the Coeur d'Alene River; dispersed camping on USFS land east of Wallace and north toward Murray or south on Big Creek Road way past the Sunshine Mine
Special attractions: Lake Coeur d'Alene Scenic Byway; Sunshine Memorial
Finding the site: From I-90, take exit 51 for Division Street and go north on Division. Turn right onto East Cameron Avenue and follow it east for 0.6 mile, then continue on Silver Valley Road for 0.8 mile as you parallel the interstate. Look for the mine on your left; there is ample parking.

Entrance to the Crystal Gold Mine tour

The air is cool underground, but it's an easy walk and a nice respite from the summer heat.

Rockhounding

It may not sound intuitive to visit a gold mine in the Silver Valley, but the Crystal Gold Mine is unique. The immediate area was mined in the 1880s, but according to the tour guide, the original owner, a miner named Tom Irwin, hid the entrance after deciding the mine wasn't good enough to keep going. He probably intended to return; many of the original tools, ore cars, and other machinery remained after he dynamited the entrance. When I-90 construction revealed a fresh spring pouring out of the mountain in 1991, a new property owner entered the picture and found the old workings. He sold the mine to Bill and Judy Lane, who developed the old workings into a tourist attraction and located some lucrative, high-paying gold ore in the quartz.

You won't see much gold in the bottom of your pan after the tour, but the polished semiprecious stones are easy for kids to pick out.

The tour itself is fascinating, and you'll get an introduction to hard-rock mining from the old hand-mining methods up to modern tools. There are interesting quartz veins on the tour that still

Iconic statue commemorating the 1972 Sunshine Mine disaster

contain wire silver and microscopic gold, and some of the walls are coated with smithsonite in multiple colors.

Outside, weather permitting, you can pan "pay dirt" for colors, but mostly what's added are polished semiprecious stones such as jasper, amethyst, and quartz. The gift shop has a good selection of books, specimens, rocks and minerals, etc.

Nearby, the Sunshine Mine Memorial is east on Silver Valley Road at 47.52806, -116.04798, at the Big Creek Road exit (exit 54) just north of the interstate. On May 2, 1972, 173 miners descended into the Sunshine Mine. Around midday, smoke started filling the air; 82 men made it to safety, while 91 miners perished from smoke inhalation. The cause was identified as most likely spontaneous combustion. The memorial, the work of sculptor Ken Lonn, commemorates the disaster.

To see the current Sunshine Mine operation, drive up Big Creek Road about 2.1 miles to 47.50156, -116.07151. Keep going and explore Big Creek; there are numerous old mines, prospects, and creeks to check.

14. Sierra Silver Mine Tour

See map on page 48.
Land type: Underground mine tour
County: Shoshone
GPS: 47.47247, -115.92481; 2,737 feet (509 Cedar St., Wallace)
Best season: May through August. Check silverminetour.org for complete schedule.
Land manager: Private
Material: Mine tour
Tools: Camera
Vehicle: Any
Accommodations: Developed camping on Coeur d'Alene Lake and north of Prichard, along the Coeur d'Alene River; dispersed camping on USFS land around Murray
Special attractions: Lake Coeur d'Alene Scenic Byway; Wallace District Mining Museum (509 Bank St., Wallace)
Finding the site: If coming from the west, take exit 61 off I-90 and continue east toward Wallace via Frontage Road/Harry F. Magnuson Way. Turn left onto Front Street/I-90 Business past the outdoor museum and drive 0.6 mile into town and to the address listed above. If coming from the east, use exit 62 and take the main road for 0.3 mile. Turn left to stay on I-90 Business to the address, about 0.5 mile.

Tour group watching the mucking operation

Rockhounding

This is another interesting, family-friendly underground tour, but with a twist. You'll start at the storefront and museum building in the middle of Wallace then ride a trolley up ID 4 a short distance to the actual mine. Along the way both to and from the actual mine, the tour guide will

High-grade silver ore from the Sierra Mine

point out interesting highlights for Wallace, such as the bordello, movie star Lana Turner's home, and more.

The underground tour of the Sierra Mine is full of the history of mining, and the operators willingly answer questions about local geology, the mineralogy at the mine, and more. This is an actual silver mine, but it was never quite profitable enough to turn into a major operation. The values were just too low—about 0.5 ounce of silver per ton. Multiple owners tried to make a go of it, but finally, in the 1960s, the mine was turned into an educational resource to train students to work in the nearby mining industry. In 1982 the nonprofit was created to turn the Sierra Mine into a tourist resource.

The gift shop and museum is a fun place to shop for souvenirs and trinkets, and there are some excellent minerals for sale, as well as inexpensive gold pans, sample ore for panning, and also plenty of books on the local history. The nearby Wallace District Mining Museum is also a must-see for rockhounds; it has plenty of rocks and minerals from the Silver Valley on display, as well as the extensive history of the mining industry here. It also has an excellent selection of books for purchase. If you ask politely for information about local rockhounding or gold panning opportunities, they'll probably send you to Prichard Creek (see Site 15).

If you want to see more sights, try the drive from Wallace north on ID 4 (past the Sierra Mine) along Canyon Creek to Gem and Burke. This little valley was the scene of repeated confrontations between miners trying to unionize and the mine owners who brought in Pinkerton security agents to infiltrate the labor ranks. A major strike in 1892 erupted into violence and brought in US Army troops after several deaths. A violent clash in 1899 arose from another strike, leading to widespread arrests. Labor unrest simmered for several years afterward.

There are several mine dumps along ID 4 for you to sample. Above Burke, the creek yields small colors. The road goes right past an old mill in Burke.

15. Prichard Creek

See map on page 48.

Land type: Large creek valley
County: Shoshone
GPS: A: 47.65781, -115.97064; 2,392 feet (Prichard Creek pull-off)
    B: 47.66157, -115.87524; 2,759 feet (Eagle Creek)
Best season: Summer through fall
Land manager: Coeur d'Alene National Forest
Material: Gold colors
Tools: Gold pan, shovel, screens
Vehicle: Any; 4WD suggested for exploring
Accommodations: Developed camping north of Prichard, along the Coeur d'Alene River; dispersed camping also available along the river
Special attractions: Extensive dredge fields in Murray
Finding the site: From Wallace, drive north on Sixth Street, under the interstate, where the road is now identified as NFD 456/Nine Mile Creek Road. Continue 10.2 miles north, where the road takes a slight right onto Beaver Creek Road; drive another 5.8 miles. Turn right onto NFD 9/Coeur D'Alene River Road and drive 1.7 miles. Cross the bridge and swing right, as if going to Murray; there is good creek access right here. To reach Site B, continue east toward Murray on NFD 9/Prichard Creek road for 2.7 miles, then turn left onto Eagle Creek Road/NFD 152. Drive 1.3 miles, stay right, and continue another 1.2 miles to the ford. A good 4WD vehicle can ford the creek during low water and continue up Eagle Creek Road for 5 miles or more, but the road washout here will stop most travelers.

Rockhounding

According to the information signs near Murray, gold was discovered near there in 1882. A. J. Prichard and his partners started prospecting near Kellogg, moved up to Beaver Creek, and actually missed the rich placer grounds at Trail Creek. They worked their way up Prichard Creek and discovered gold near what is now Murray. They swore one another to secrecy, but the news inevitably spilled out, and soon 5,000 miners descended. The primitive camp at Eagle was soon overtaken by the better locale at Murray. Prospecting continued and worked the south fork of the Coeur d'Alene River, eventually resulting in discovery of the major silver-lead deposits in Silver Valley.

The ford at Eagle Creek. Drive across, take a hard left, and resume traveling north—if necessary.

The Prichard Creek site has easy access, and you could scout all the way to the Coeur d'Alene River if you wanted to. This site was claimed when gold prices were extremely high but was open more recently. The dredge fields at Murray worked Prichard Creek extensively, and you can still see the stacked rows from the dredge. Down this far from Murray, you should have no trouble recovering black sands and small colors, with an occasionally larger flake if you can dig down. Be sure to fill in your holes. If the site is claimed, scout around on just about any creek, try the river, or move on to Site B.

Site B is on Eagle Creek, at the site of a major washout. Even if the road is fixed in the future, this is still a good place to check. There have been placer mines farther up Eagle Creek in the past, so, as usual with gold panning, be on the lookout for claim markers.

If you're frustrated by meager results and want to continue prospecting, your best bet, especially if gold prices have jumped dramatically, is to join up with a local or national gold-mining club and thus gain access to their claims inventory. For example, the Gold Prospectors Association of America (GPAA) has maintained a claim up on Prichard Creek and another on Eagle Creek past Site B.

16. St. Joe River

See map on page 48.
Land type: Forested riverbanks and creek beds
County: Shoshone
GPS: A: 47.19101, -115.49791; 3,033 feet (Bluff Creek)
  B: 47.15815, -115.41599; 3,315 feet (Conrad Campground)
  C: 47.15088, -115.40742; 3,348 feet (Gold Creek)
Best season: Late summer
Land manager: USDA Forest Service–St. Joe National Forest
Material: Gold and tumbler material
Tools: Gold pan, screens, shovel, geology pick
Vehicle: Any; roads mostly paved; 4WD required if exploring off main road or past end of pavement
Accommodations: Developed camping plentiful along the river to the east; primitive campgrounds on national forest lands throughout this area
Special attractions: St. Joe River Scenic Byway; Avery work center historical site
Finding the site: The small town of Avery sits on the St. Joe River, about 46 miles from St. Maries. From Avery take St. Joe River Road/NFD 50 about 21.3 miles to reach a slim pull-out on the inside bend of the river. This is Site A. Conrad Crossing Campground is Site B; drive 6.9 miles farther up the road. The junction with Gold Creek Road/NFD 388 is just 0.8 mile farther.

Rockhounding

Check for quartzite, jasper, and other interesting rock wherever you can reach the river. The gravels contain a nice tan jasper, and the quartz is leaning to agate. There are faint traces of gold on the St. Joe River, so if you find a good trap or crevice to clean out, try it. There are more mines up the North Fork of the St. Joe River, on NFD 456.

If you just want a taste and don't have time to drive way up the river, you can still find good gravels at 47.24745, -116.01265, about 34.7 miles up the St. Joe River from St. Maries. Long ago there was a lode mine near here for copper, silver, and gold—the Kelly Mine, across the river but long gone. But to really get a taste of remote Idaho, you should drive farther up to Site A.

Extensive gravel bars on the St. Joe River contain quartz and spotty jasper; check the head of these gravel bars for tiny garnets and trace amounts of gold.

At one time there was a small underground mine here across the river—the St. Joe Quartz Mine, with gold and copper. It seems to be overtaken by nature—I didn't spot any traces. Still, you can locate some inside bends along this stretch and dig deep down. Just be sure to refill your holes, here and elsewhere.

Site B is near the Conrad Crossing prospect, another of the area's ubiquitous copper and gold diggings. Across the river somewhere was the Whitetail prospect; if you get a chance to chip away at outcrops in the area, you might be able to start with malachite and work your way to quartz with rusty staining. The panning in this particular area is pretty good; you should be able to get to black sands and small colors of gold with no trouble. There are no coordinates for it that look reliable, but it was somewhere on the hillside above the campground. The campground is a good base camp to scout out unoccupied inside bends near here that you can reach when the water is low. Also, at the bridge across the St. Joe, cross over and drive about 0.6 mile up NFD 509. The Bluff Creek Copper Claim is at 47.18067, -115.4943.

Site C is the intersection with Gold Creek. You can check around the creek mouth for good gravity traps, or even journey up Gold Creek.

If you really want to prospect this area, the best location for gold is probably on remote Heller Creek, way up at the top of the St. Joe River. This spot is past Red Ives on NFD 320; the coordinates are 47.06415, -115.21924. There are numerous abandoned claims and old workings here—it's the headwaters of the St. Joe, and just down the ridge from the Montana border. I have still never been there, so I can't vouch for the roads, which I imagine are little more than jeep trails.

This is one of the most picturesque drives in Idaho, and very far off the beaten path. Everyone I've taken up here was smitten with the area. Deer are everywhere, especially along the road, and it is very important that you slow down, particularly during those hours at the end of the day when deer head for their last drink of water before bedding down. Most of the campgrounds we passed were completely empty.

17. Big Carpenter Creek

See map on page 61.

Land type: Road cuts

County: Benewah

GPS: A: 47.07151, -116.38374; 2,899 feet (first spot)

B: 47.05828, -116.39631; 2,803 feet (middle spot)

C: 47.05767, -116.41678; 2,920 feet (farthest spot)

Best season: Year-round, except dead of winter

Land manager: Benewah County (road); USDA Forest Service–St. Joe National Forest

Material: Staurolite crosses (extremely rare), occasional single staurolite crystals, plentiful garnet

Tools: Hammer, chisels

Vehicle: Any, though the gravel road is bumpy.

Accommodations: Developed camping at Emerald Creek; primitive camping on nearby national forest lands, especially around the Palouse River. There are lots of camping spots throughout the area, but pay attention to fences, gates, and posted areas.

There's plenty of staurolite schist and garnet schist to break up along upper Big Carpenter Creek.

Sites 17–22

Special attractions: White Pine Scenic Byway

Finding the site: Drive south on ID 3 from Fernwood, but before leaving town completely, look for Carpenter Creek Road to the right. You can tell you're on the correct road if you crossed the railroad tracks and the St. Maries River and drove past the Dumpster site. The side road to the right that follows Little Carpenter Creek Road is marked, but the right turn that stays on Carpenter Creek Road has no sign, nor does the road that continues on to Emerald Creek. About 1.9 miles from Fernwood, turn right to stay on Carpenter Creek Road. From the turn, Site A is about 1.4 miles, Site B is about 2.7 miles, and Site C is about 3.7 miles.

Rockhounding

Search throughout the tailings in the cuts for small, dark crystals of staurolite, an iron-aluminum-zinc silicate hydroxide. The crystals tend to be short and stubby, and not always well-formed. What you really want are twinned crystals at 90-degree angles, forming a cross. These are now very rare—Beckwith's 1972 book (see bibliography) has lured a lot of rockhounds here over the years. You might have to settle for simple crystals in clusters and lots of garnet.

The heavily worked cuts at Site A and Site B offer easier opportunities to bust up rocks. With patience and luck, you might be rewarded with a staurolite cross. If not, you should at least get some display-worthy garnet schist.

We looked over Little Carpenter Creek, which Beckwith lists, but we think that was an error on his map. Listed above are three large cuts to explore along the main Carpenter Creek, and they match his mileage. Unfortunately, the staurolite crosses are very rare. Miners dredge commercial quantities of garnet in this drainage, so the creek bed is claimed. Stay off their property and out of their way.

Schist at Big Carpenter Creek is loaded with garnets, but there is also rare staurolite.

18. Emerald Creek

See map on page 61.

Land type: Forested creek bed operated as fee dig, plus road cut
County: Latah
GPS: A: 46.99607, -116.36467; 2,916 feet (fee dig)
    B: 46.99120, -116.36750; 2,345 feet (road cut)
Best season: Generally open Memorial Day through Labor Day; check www.fs
.usda.gov/recarea/ipnf/recarea/?recid=6927 for details.
Land manager: USDA Forest Service–St. Joe National Forest
Material: World-class star garnet
Tools: Provided after paying the fee
Vehicle: Any
Accommodations: Developed camping at Emerald Creek Campground; primitive camping up NFD 447
Special attractions: White Pine Scenic Byway; fee-based fossil dig at the Clarkia Race Track; Elk River Back Country Byway
Finding the site: From Fernwood, drive south on ID 3 about 4.4 miles to Emerald Creek Road/NFD 447 and turn right (west). You can also reach this turn by driving about 5.5 miles north from Clarkia. The parking area is about 7.2 miles from the highway on an excellent road.

Rockhounding

This garnet-collecting area has undergone many changes over the years. At one time, rockhounds could drive right up, slop around in the muddy creek, and pull up very large garnets for their efforts. No Name Gulch, Garnet Gulch, and 281 Gulch were all easy to access and plentiful. It was common to see someone working every creek before it plunged under the road and into Emerald Creek. I remember seeing entire families playing around in the creek bottom at 281 Gulch and eating their picnic lunch in the shade. By July 2008 the number of folks looking for star garnets had increased to the point where the USFS set a cap of 170 people per day. Next, the garnet area was completely transformed and made essentially wheelchair accessible. There was a modest 0.5-mile hike from the parking area (following the signs), but if you had folks with mobility issues along, you could hike up ahead to ask a ranger to come down and unlock the gate for the quick drive.

Washing gravels for star garnets at the Emerald Creek fee-dig area

By 2019 the site had been shut down, as the forest service had run out of pay dirt. There were reports that this site might be resurrected, but the folks at Fossil Bowl told me they were strongly considering starting up their own fee-dig operation.

It's not a good sign that the operation was even paused; there should be plenty of material in this drainage. Call the St. Maries Office at (208) 245-2531 for up-to-date information and to possibly secure a garnet digging permit, if they are still being issued.

I have seen cars with license plates from Florida, Minnesota, New York, and other far-flung places in the parking lot, so believe it when this is referred to as a world-class garnet area. The trick is to find a garnet big enough to polish with the "star" showing, the site's star attraction.

Pea-size garnets are common in Emerald Creek, but there are some monsters in the area too.

Site B is just down the road from the parking area, about 0.5 mile at most. The road cut contains ample exposures of garnet-bearing schist that makes for an interesting display piece. Park carefully and be quick here, and watch for traffic along this road.

Note: To protect fish habitat, you are forbidden from digging in the creek with tools to recover garnets.

19. Bechtel Mountain

See map on page 61.
Land type: Mountaintop
County: Shoshone
GPS: 46.99125, -116.31863; 4,583 feet
Best season: Summer through early fall
Land manager: USDA Forest Service–St. Joe National Forest
Material: Garnets
Tools: Hammer, trowel
Vehicle: Any
Accommodations: Developed camping at Emerald Creek Campground; primitive camping on national forest lands to the west. I've seen fire rings at the very top of the mountain.

Nice view from the top of Bechtel Mountain; the rocks at the top are full of fragments.

Special attractions: Elk River Back Country Byway; Fossil Bowl

Finding the site: From Fernwood, drive south on ID 3 about 4.4 miles to Emerald Creek Road/NFD 447 and turn right (west). Drive about 4.7 miles, then turn left onto Fossil Road/NFD 504. Drive 1.5 miles and take a sharp right onto Bechtel Mountain Road. From Clarkia on ID 3, drive south 1.3 miles to Fossil Road and turn right (west). Drive about 2.3 miles and turn onto Bechtel Mountain Road. Continue for 4 miles; stay on the main road and you'll reach the top.

Rockhounding

With the Emerald Creek fee-dig in suspended mode, I added this site because you won't go home skunked—and it's nearby. The last bit of the road to the very top may tax a 2WD vehicle, but it's doable. The geology is the same as for Emerald Creek, with significant exposures of almandine garnet schist all the way to the top of the road. There are reports that these garnets also show the star pattern if polished correctly to display the inclusions within.

There are some old diggings along the logging road to the right at 46.98594, -116.32169. Look for more faint trails with recent activity off this road, as there are bound to be more diggings for bigger garnets. The top is more reliable for the view and for smaller garnets. Fisher shows a site at the end of the logging road.

This road is called Fossil Road for a reason. There's a good road cut worth checking out at 47.00869, -116.31144, but since nearby Fossil Bowl is so much better, I'm just mentioning it here. You could certainly explore for more fossils and more schist outcrops in this area.

Be on your best defensive alert when driving ID 3—it is feared locally for devastating moose-car collisions. Plenty of deer roam the nearby hills as well, and they're almost as dangerous because they often wait until the last second to leap out in front of you. Use caution.

The rubble below the outcrops at the top is full of garnets eroded from the schist.

20. Hoodoo Placers

See map on page 61.

Land type: River bottom, tailings

County: Latah

GPS: A: 46.96613, -116.56876; 2,860 feet (lower area)

    B: 47.01084, -116.53436; 3,272 feet (Mary Lee placer)

Best season: Spring through fall; best at low water

Land manager: USDA Forest Service–Clearwater National Forest

Material: Gold, garnet; tumbler material

Tools: Gold-panning equipment

Vehicle: 4WD suggested; gravel roads get dusty, and washboards are common.

Accommodations: Developed camping at Emerald Creek and along White Pine Drive; primitive camping on national forest lands all along the North Fork

Special attractions: White Pine Scenic Byway; Moose Meadows; Mica Mountain

Finding the site: From Harvard (about 60 miles northeast of Lewiston), at the intersection of ID 6 and ID 9, head 3.6 miles northeast on ID 6. Turn right (east) onto NFD 447/Palouse River Road and drive 6.6 miles to the intersection with NFD 767. This is where the Palouse is joined by the North Fork of the Palouse River. To reach here from the Clarkia area, drive 5.5 north on ID 3, turn left onto NFD 447, and drive 19 miles west on the main road. This general area is Site A. To reach Site B, turn right (north) onto NFD 767 and travel through the tailings about 3.8 miles, to the junction with NFD 1423.

Rockhounding

This area is wide open for gold panning, sluicing, and searching for tumbler material and mineralization. It was prospected long ago, saw a slight resurgence in the Depression years, and has been half-dormant ever since. If gold goes up to $2,000 per ounce, it's possible that the area could see some renewed interest, but all the easy stuff is gone. If you see new claim posts in the area, be flexible and move around. The gold was never that great in this area, so it's hard to imagine that the Hoodoo Placers will see a major resurgence. That still leaves a lot of fine gold and small flakes for weekenders.

The kids will like playing around on the big dredge tailings piles and mounds of round river rock. I enjoy working the river bars and gravel banks, adding to my concentrate collection. I found abundant black sand and lots of

Extensive placer operations dot the 4-mile stretch from the bottom of the North Fork of the Palouse River.

garnet in just about every sample. I also picked up some material from the creek, breaking out some good specimen rocks with garnet in the schist and sulfides, such as pyrite, in the matrix.

Site A has good gravel, as does another big flat, open spot less than 0.5 mile downstream called the Poorman Placer at 46.96951, -116.58421. Site B, about 3.8 miles up the North Fork of the Palouse, reaches the northern extent of the mineralization here. Check as many drainages as you have time for as you reach Site B; there is mineralization in these hills on both sides of the valley.

This district is a great example of hydrothermal alteration—the basement rocks have been heated and repeatedly injected with hot, watery quartz veins. The old literature (now out of print) lists malachite, azurite, cuprite, pyrrhotite, arsenopyrite, bornite, chalcopyrite, pyrite, and tourmaline in the hard rock mines around here. Take your time and look for a good showpiece with lots of mineralization, but be advised that some were identified using X-ray diffraction. I included the Mizpah site in the first edition, but when I checked back on it, the road in was almost completely overgrown.

Vuggy quartz with mineralization from the North Fork of the Palouse. I've busted up samples like this with a hammer and panned colors.

21. Fossil Bowl

See map on page 61.
Land type: Large cut behind a popular motocross speedway
County: Shoshone
GPS: 46.99121, -116.27737; 2,882 feet
Best season: Summer through early fall
Land manager: Privately held by the Keinbaum family
Material: Miocene leaf fossils
Tools: Chisels and blades for splitting siltstone
Vehicle: Any
Accommodations: None at site; developed camping at Emerald Creek
Campground; primitive camping on national forest lands to the west
Special attractions: Elk River Back Country Byway; Gold Bug Mine on Jerome
Creek Road
Finding the site: Fossil Bowl is located on ID 3, about 1.6 miles south of Clarkia or
13.4 miles north of Bovill. You can't miss the motorcycle track on the west side of
the road.

Fossil leaves are abundant at Fossil Bowl's fee-dig locale.

Rockhounding

This kid-friendly fee site is located in the cliffs behind a motocross track. There is a nice shade awning over the fossil site, so the sun doesn't completely burn you out.

The fossils here are typical of a *lagerstätte,* where deep lake waters, lack of oxygen, and fast accumulation of sediments combined to exquisitely preserve and concentrate delicate fossils. Miocene in age, or about 15 million years old, the beds contain mostly leaves, but fish fossils have been collected from the deposit. Because this is private land, the usual restrictions on collecting vertebrates don't apply.

When these fossils were laid down, the local environment resembled a Florida swamp, with an amazing diversity of foliage. Paleontologists have identified at least 125 plant species at Clarkia. Scientists have long flocked here to study the plants, and they have recently extracted DNA from the plant material.

The leaves are preserved so completely that you need to take precautions as you split the rock and reveal the contents. Exposure to air will quickly turn the green fossils brown or black, so the Fossil Bowl organizers recommend that you quickly wrap your new treasure in wet newspaper and then seal it in a plastic bag. The newspaper will slowly draw moisture from the matrix, drying the sample and ensuring that the fossil itself remains. It can take several weeks or even months to cure the specimens.

Fossil fragments abound in the rubble below the main dig area, but better specimens come from splitting rock. Old knives are provided!

The owners here are super helpful and have handouts showing the most common leaves. They'll get the kids started, and they have a few tools if you don't bring any. (Note: If it's a busy day with several families, there won't be enough hammers, so bring one if you plan ahead.) The usual caution about using common carpentry hammers for rockhounding doesn't apply here; you're just tapping with an old knife, not whacking quartzite.

22. Mica Mountain

See map on page 61.
Land type: Forested mountaintop pit mine
County: Latah
GPS: A: 46.88581, -116.57491; 3,456 feet (turn)
     B: 46.88722, -116.57546; 4,281 feet (pits)
Best season: Early summer through early fall
Land manager: USDA Forest Service–Clearwater National Forest
Material: Mica, tourmaline, rare beryl
Tools: Geology pick or heavy hammer

Search for black tourmaline (schorl) crystals on the left side of this little gully at the top of Mica Mountain. Big sheets of mica are common, and elusive beryl crystals hide in the big pegmatite boulders.

Vehicle: 4WD suggested

Accommodations: Primitive camping throughout the area as you get closer to the mountaintop; more good camping along the creek on the road up the mountain. The Potlatch River has developed camping.

Special attractions: Elk River Back Country Byway; Moscow isn't too far away.

Finding the site: From Deary, head west on ID 8 about 0.8 mile and turn right (north) onto ID 9. Drive about 2.3 miles and turn right onto Mica Mountain Road, which is marked with a sign. At 1.8 miles look alert: I've missed this turn twice. A faint road leads off to the right, but it "feels" like you want to stay on Old Avon Road. Don't do it—take the right turn. About 0.8 mile up, a left-hand turn will tempt you, but stay on the main track. Another 0.9 mile up there is a new shortcut, but it feels better to stay on Mica Mountain Road. After another 5.3 miles, about 7 miles total, mostly up, from ID 9, there is a tempting option to take a left; don't. Drive another 0.3 mile to Site A, which is the coordinates for a left turn. We drove our Jeep a short ways and parked, so you may want to just park at Site A. Walk in and stay right; if you go left, which leads down the hill, you'll soon spot rusting equipment—including a big chute—that looks to be from the 1970s. A trail goes past these relics and joins back up to the road. Instead, follow the ATV tracks to the cliffs and the cut where the tourmaline crystals litter the hillside at Site B.

Rockhounding

The industrial use of mica ended years ago; it used to show up as flame-proof "isinglass" windows in wood stoves. The size of the mica "books" here will astound you—4 inches isn't unheard of, and bigger pieces are still possible. After you get good representative samples of mica out of the way, start looking for the tourmaline. The small black crystals erode continually and are easy to pick up. It is actually more interesting to get them in matrix, as they so quickly fall out. Some are fragile, but look for big fatties almost as big around as a pencil. My favorites showed terminations on both ends and cleaned up nicely. Kids will love this crystal experience.

Faint green beryl is hard to find; don't expect to see it. You would have to get the sweet spot on the pegmatite vein and then hack out some fresh material. Unfortunately, that vein is high up the cliff. Beryl hunters have haunted this mountaintop for decades and have scoured the dumps, so be on the lookout for faint green beryl as you split open chunks of rock, but be skeptical about finding any.

Large "books" of muscovite mica are easy to spot all over the top of Mica Mountain.

Fragile, slender black tourmaline (schorl) crystals, loose and in mica schist

A couple of us hiked all the way to the top of nearby Potato Hill, out of Deary, but didn't find any agate. Maybe there was a seam there once, as described in some old books, but we didn't see any sign of recent diggings. Some maps show more mines near Mica Mountain, but getting there seems challenging with these roads. A better bet would be to check out Gold Hill, north of Harvard at 46.96381, -116.74780; the Copper Ridge prospect, Gold Bug prospect, Gold Hill prospect, and other locales await. Refer to "Minerals of Latah County" for more information.

23. Freezeout Ridge

See map on page 75.

Land type: Alpine forest, ridgetop

County: Shoshone

GPS: A: 47.00825, -116.02996; 5,961 feet (garnet)

      B: 47.00485, -116.02909; 5,909 feet (kyanite)

      C: 47.00303, -116.02917; 5,942 feet (garnet)

Best season: Late summer

Land manager: USDA Forest Service–St. Joe National Forest

Search the outcrops at Freezeout Ridge for garnets and kyanite.

Sites 23–27

Material: Kyanite, garnet
Tools: Heavy hammer, strong chisels
Vehicle: Strong 4WD required
Accommodations: Primitive camping here and throughout national forest lands in the area
Special attractions: St. Joe River Scenic Byway; Dismal Lake; Hobo Botanical Area
Finding the site: From ID 3, just north of the Fossil Bowl, exit to Clarkia. This is Main Street. Drive through what's left of the town and bear right as the road becomes Poplar Street. Go 0.4 mile and turn left onto NFD 321. Take this road, which is excellent, for 0.9 mile and turn right onto NFD 301. Follow NFD 301 for 14.3 miles, past the St. Maries River, where the road worsens, until you get to the saddle at Freezeout. Turn onto NFD 384 and pause. There is a smaller track going off to the left, leading to a good fire pit and a rickety picnic table. The road to the right leads to Site A (0.6 mile, on the left), Site B (0.8 mile, on the left), and Site C (1.1 miles, on the right).

The drive is even tougher as you head farther east. A sturdy rig can make the trip from here to NFD 201 and thus over to Bathtub Mountain (or Avery), but you'll need four-wheel drive, excellent (at least 8-ply) tires, sturdy suspension, plenty of gas, and lots of time. Also, plan your trip carefully. We ran into a solid snowbank all the way across the road in late June one year and had to turn back. Another time, we confronted a diminished, receding bank of frosty ice in early August that prompted everyone to get out of the rig, re-ice the coolers, then turn around.

Rockhounding

Freezeout Ridge is metamorphosed beyond belief. If you remember your geology, as shale is continually cooked, it transitions like this: shale > mica schist > garnet schist > staurolite schist > kyanite schist > sillimanite. Then it becomes a gneiss. This locale has been hit hard, but there is still material present. There are pale kyanite crystals in some of the rocks. Garnet crystals show up throughout the schist here, and we found some really large garnets— plum-size—throughout the area. You might be able to dig some out around the richer outcrops. Site A offers a lot of garnets, mostly in display pieces. Site C contains large samples of plain, massive quartz, mostly lying on the surface, plus more garnets as you head south. In addition, there's a great view.

Large garnet crystals poke out of a boulder on Freezeout Ridge.

The bladed kyanite crystals are across the road at Site B—take a few minutes to start identifying. Look for garnets here as well, but the kyanite is the main prize. Kyanite is difficult to extract from the matrix—strive mainly for specimen samples. The crystals tend to interlock and can be quite striking, but you won't find much material eroded out of the matrix and sitting on top of the soil. This is heavy hammer work, so bring a big one.

Fisher (see bibliography) also reports huckleberries in season and lake fishing in this area.

24. Crater Peak

See map on page 75.

Land type: Alpine forest, ridgetop

County: Shoshone

GPS: A: 47.02478, -115.98748; 6,212 feet (garnet)

B: 47.02723, -115.98371; 6,318 feet (camp)

C: 47.03098, -115.98333; 6,290 feet (garnet)

Best season: Late summer

Land manager: USDA Forest Service–St. Joe National Forest

Material: Garnet

Tools: Shovel

Vehicle: Strong 4WD required

Accommodations: Primitive camping at Site B and throughout national forest lands in the area

The pit at Site A contains loose garnets, making for easy extraction.

Special attractions: St. Joe River Scenic Byway; Dismal Lake; Hobo Botanical Area

Finding the site: From ID 3, just north of the Fossil Bowl, exit to Clarkia. This is Main Street. Drive through what's left of the town and bear right as the road turns into Poplar Street. Go 0.4 mile and turn left onto NFD 321. Take this road, which is excellent, for 0.9 mile and turn right onto NFD 301. This bridge marks the old mining camp of Gold Center. Follow NFD 301 for 16.5 miles, past the saddle at Freezeout Ridge (Site 23). You'll see some signs of digging on the left (upper) side of the road at Site A. Continue 0.3 mile to the campgrounds at Site B, and another 0.3 mile to the second pits, Site C.

Rockhounding

You won't find many garnet locales that are easier than this. The hard part is locating the pits, as they can be tricky at first. If you've reached the campgrounds at Site B, you've gone too far. Look above the road for signs of digging, and locate the large pit that has been steadily widened over the years. If you look closely, you'll see roundish, orange

Modest collection of loose garnets dug from Site A

rocks. Pick them up, brush off the soil that clings to them, and you should soon identify crystal faces of a dodecahedron, or twelve-sided crystal.

You can scrape the walls of the pit, which contain a lot of decomposing mica, and pick out more garnets. You want to concentrate your efforts on the best-shaped specimens, and the bigger, the better. Don't go too crazy—it would be good if these two pits last for years to come. The garnet schist is decomposing slowly but surely in this area, so you could probably scout out more outcrops to dig into.

Be sure to practice good manners here. In addition to leaving some garnets for the next adventuresome soul who braves NF 301, don't leave rocks in the road, pick up any trash you see, and leave the site better than when you found it.

25. Bathtub Mountain

See map on page 75.

Land type: Small cut along trail in alpine forest
County: Shoshone
GPS: 47.07588, -115.55982; 5,589 feet
Best season: August; avoid threat of snow.
Land manager: USDA Forest Service–St. Joe National Forest
Material: Staurolite crystals, some twinned; garnet
Tools: Heavy hammer, chisels
Vehicle: 4WD required; roads are extremely rough in places.
Accommodations: Primitive camping at trailhead; developed campground at Mammoth Springs
Special attractions: Dismal Lake
Finding the site: From ID 3, just north of the Fossil Bowl, exit to Clarkia. This is Main Street. Drive through what's left of the town and bear right as the road turns into Poplar Street. Go 0.4 mile and turn left onto NFD 321. Take this road, which is excellent, for 0.9 mile and turn right onto NFD 301. This bridge marks the old mining camp of Gold Center. Follow NFD 301 for 33.8 miles, past the saddle at Freezeout (Site 23) and past the diggings at Crater Peak (Site 24). At Jungle Creek Road, turn sharply right and drive 6.4 miles to a right turn onto NFD 201. Stay on NFD 201 for 24.2 miles to the coordinates. You can also come in from Avery by taking the St. Joe River Road for 22.1 miles to NFD 509 and drive 11.2 miles. Turn left onto NFD 201 and drive 4.4 miles to the Trail 100 trailhead, which leads to the coordinates.

Rockhounding

After driving so far to reach this spot, the collecting locale is relatively easy to find. Hike down Trail 100 to the small flat outcrop where rockhounds have chipped up the schist bearing the staurolite on the left side of the trail. There is a very large boulder of staurolite schist off to the left as well, and plenty more up the hill to the top of the ridge. We spent quite a bit of time hammering at the schist for specimen samples, and also looked around in the dust for crystals that had eroded out of matrix. The staurolite is a dark brown when fresh, regularly up to 1 inch long and sometimes longer. It is rarely twinned, but

Staurolite-bearing schist from Bathtub Mountain, with some loose crystals

that's the challenge: The twinning can occur as interesting 60- and 90-degree crosses, and there are rare three-pronged clusters (Ream 2012, 53). Try to make time to find the best crystals, because this might be an area you only visit once in your rockhounding career.

There are reports of staurolite sites just south of Avery, but I haven't stopped at enough of the road cuts to track the Avery spots down. Many rocks out here contain garnet, so be on the lookout for that mineral as well.

Snow is an issue up here until early July in some years, starting again probably in mid-September, depending on the year. It took me three tries to reach this locale because I stubbornly tried too early in the year. One more note of caution: Avoid trying to reach this site from Freezeout Ridge with the wrong vehicle. The first 5 miles or so from Freezeout, headed east, are atrocious, and in some spots it gets even worse. We crawled along at less than 5 miles per hour and truly wished we had driven back to Clarkia and around to the St. Joe River; that trip is about 38 miles, with part of it paved. It can take 4 hours to reach Bathtub Mountain from Freezeout Ridge, for example. Mammoth Springs is a good campground, so that helps.

26. Blackdome Peak

See map on page 75.

Land type: Alpine forest, ridgetop

County: Shoshone

GPS: 46.98934, -115.84278; 6,055 feet (garnet)

Best season: Late summer

Land manager: USDA Forest Service–St. Joe National Forest

Material: Kyanite, garnet

Tools: Heavy hammer, strong chisels

Vehicle: Strong 4WD required

Accommodations: Primitive camping here and throughout national forest lands in the area

Special attractions: St. Joe River Scenic Byway; Dismal Lake; Hobo Botanical Area

Finding the site: From ID 3, just north of the Fossil Bowl, exit to Clarkia. This is Main Street. Drive through what's left of the town and bear right as the road turns

Kyanite-studded boulder near Blackdome Peak

into Poplar Street. Go 0.4 mile and turn left onto NFD 321. Take this road, which is excellent, for 0.9 mile and turn right onto NFD 301. Follow NFD 301 for 24.7 miles, past the saddle at Freezeout Ridge (Site 23), past the garnets at Site 24, and past the turn to Bathtub Mountain (Site 25). Turn right onto Indian Dip Road and follow it for 4.4 miles to the coordinates.

Rockhounding

Blackdome Ridge shows increasing metamorphism from the garnet locales at Bathtub Mountain and Crater Peak. This kyanite is present as striking lumps on the large boulders, and loose crystals are common in the road. The kyanite is not the striking blue you often see in rock shops; it is paler, although some crystals are a light blue. Kyanite is common in what's known as a blueschist terrain, and you'll start seeing a blue tint to the rocks as you near Goat Mountain and the turn to Blackdome Peak. The crystals at the coordinates are dense and hard to dislodge from the boulder, so your best bet is to scout for eroded crystals.

There is more garnet near the bottom of the road to Blackdome Peak, and we hiked it for a ways. It took two tries to reach this locale; the first trip in early July was blocked by snow, but the road was clear three weeks later. The collecting season for this area can be as short as a few months. Still, if you can mount a "super-trip" and hit Freezeout Ridge, Crater Peak, Bathtub Mountain, Blackdome Peak, and O'Donnell Creek in one outing, you'll feel pretty good.

Kyanite is an interesting mineral for trying a hardness test. It will show two different hardness scores, depending on whether you scratch it with the striations or along them. Ream (2012, 136) notes that geology students from neighboring universities study here, and thus limit your collecting along the road. It's a pleasant area to roam around, so that shouldn't be a problem.

Loose kyanite crystals collected from the road and the soil around the large boulders

27. O'Donnell Creek

See map on page 75.
Land type: Alpine forest, ridgetop
County: Shoshone
GPS: 46.97480, -115.88081; 4,170 feet (garnet)
Best season: Late summer
Land manager: USDA Forest Service–St. Joe National Forest
Material: Kyanite, garnet
Tools: Heavy hammer, strong chisels
Vehicle: Strong 4WD required
Accommodations: Primitive camping here and throughout national forest lands in the area
Special attractions: St. Joe River Scenic Byway; Dismal Lake; Hobo Botanical Area
Finding the site: From ID 3, just north of the Fossil Bowl, exit to Clarkia. This is Main Street. Drive through what's left of the town and bear right as the road turns into Poplar Street. Go 0.4 mile and turn left onto NFD 321. Take this road, which is excellent, for 0.9 mile and turn right onto NFD 301. Follow NFD 301 for 24.7 miles, past the saddle at Freezeout Ridge (Site 23), past the garnets at Site 24, and past the turn to Bathtub Mountain (Site 25). Turn right onto Indian Dip Road and follow it for 5.2 miles, then turn right onto NFD 457. Stay on this road for 5.3 miles to the coordinates. Note: You could have turned at Gold Center and driven on NFD 457 all the way, but you would have missed the metamorphic rocks in the last several sites.

Rockhounding

This quartz crystal locale used to be claimed and specimens were offered for sale along the road near Clarkia, but the site is now open again. The crystals that are easiest to locate are loose on the ground at the diggings, but you can also dig for bigger specimens. The main diggings are above the road, and the faint trail takes a minute to locate. You'll soon pop into an obvious dug-up area, however. You can choose to expand an existing hole or start one on your own. You can follow one of the trenches as well. Digging could reward you with clusters of excellent crystals 2 to 3 inches in length once you locate the zone in the bedrock where they are most common. The crystals can be

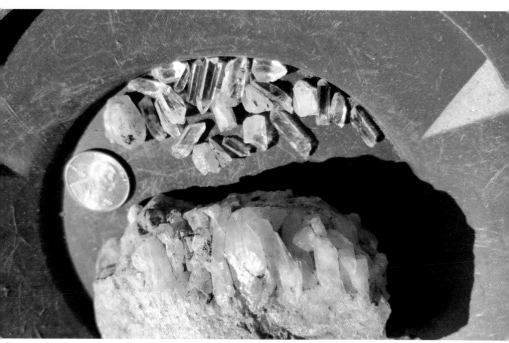

Assortment of small quartz crystals from surface collecting at O'Donnell Creek's upper pits

excellent quality, sometimes completely clear with beautiful terminations. If you can spend time here, you should be rewarded, but plan on hard work if you do any digging. Be sure to remove trash when you leave, because if the site builds up with garbage, rockhounds could lose it.

28. Orofino Creek

See map on page 87.

Land type: Old mine, forested creek bed
County: Clearwater
GPS: 46.50558, -115.88254; 2,721 feet (Orofino Creek)
Best season: Late summer; low water required
Land manager: USDA Forest Service–Clearwater National Forest
Material: Gold ore in quartz at the mine. Pan for gold and garnets from the creek, and keep an eye out for tumbler material in the creek and tributaries. There are reports of rare green epidote and gray to blue sapphire.
Tools: Geology pick, gold pan, screens, shovel
Vehicle: 4WD suggested for gravel roads
Accommodations: Primitive camping throughout this area on national forest lands; developed camping at Dworshak Reservoir

Orofino Creek contains tiny red garnets, small green crystals of epidote, plus rare bronze and blue sapphires.

Sites 28–30, 32

Special attractions: Gold Rush Historic Byway; Dworshak Dam; Dent Bridge

Finding the site: From Pierce, drive north on ID 11/Main Street for 3.9 miles. Turn west onto Canal Street and drive 3.9 miles; turn left, drive 3.1 miles, then take a slight left and continue 2.1 miles. Park safely near the bridge over Orofino Creek.

Rockhounding

At the bridge, look around along the creek for quartz with rusty staining, quartz with dark inclusions, and quartz with visible pyrite. We found material in the creek itself and along the trails and roads throughout this area. Orofino Creek was a big gold producer in its day, and anywhere you can get access is likely to pay off. Some of its tributaries could surprise you as well. The creek crossing offers a couple of options. You can pan here if the water is low enough, and you'll see dredge tailings and ponds throughout the area to inspire you. Small roads can get you in closer to the creek and upstream on either side from the bridge, but it depends on the weather, your vehicle, and your desire. There is a nice oxbow up the creek about 0.4 mile east of the bridge, accessible via a path from the north side. As usual, check for claim markers and be flexible with changing land ownership, but this area hasn't seen a claim marker in the last ten years that I've visited.

Save all your black sands and concentrates and check them with a hand lens. Green epidote is a possibility up here, and some sources mention sapphire. There are some striking red ochre deposits in this region, and there is at least one deposit on the road into Orofino Creek.

29. Pierce

See map on page 87.

Land type: Creek beds

County: Clearwater

GPS: A: 46.45483, -115.77534; 3,601 feet (Orofino Creek)
B: 46.46554, -115.72121; 3,547 feet (Rosebud Creek)

Best season: Summer; wait for low water.

Land manager: USDA Forest Service–Clearwater National Forest

Material: Gold, almandine garnet; decent shot at sapphire and epidote; also tumbler material

Tools: Gold pan, screens, shovels; heavy hammer to break up rocks

Vehicle: 4WD suggested

Accommodations: Developed camping at Clearwater Gulch, Hollywood Campground near Pierce, Weitas Creek Campground on the North Fork of the Clearwater; dispersed camping along French Creek, Orogrande Creek, and elsewhere on USFS land

Special attractions: Gold Rush Historic Byway. Pierce has an excellent prospecting shop and full services; check the Pierce discovery site and museum.

Finding the site: From Carle Street in Pierce, drive south on ID 11 about 0.8 mile. Turn left onto French Mountain Road/CR 250; drive about 2.4 miles and park carefully. The creek is accessible here. To reach Site B, drive 2.8 miles farther on French Mountain Road to where Road 5170 veers off to the creek; there are several bridges to check and access to both Rosebud and Orofino Creeks.

Rockhounding

Pierce is the site of the first major gold discovery way back in the summer of 1862, in what was then the Idaho Territory. Thousands of miners soon flocked to Orofino Creek and worked the surrounding hillsides. Of course the easy gold is long gone, but don't think there's nothing left—modern equipment, with its sharp riffles and "miner's moss" in the sluice, can catch material with far more efficiency. Expect mostly flour gold with small flakes, but there is still a chance of finding decent-size gold if you can hit the right crevice. Be sure to save your concentrates and black sands to inspect with a powerful hand lens. Micro prizes include red garnet, green epidote, and rare bluish sapphire.

Pierce Hardware has a great prospecting mural.

The Idaho Batholith and Belt Series of metamorphosed sediments underlie this district. Quartz veins with pyrite, arsenopyrite, and free gold occur near bodies of gneiss and are associated with pegmatite, diabase, and aplite dikes.

The best places to find heavy material such as gold, garnet, and sapphire are where the creek makes a sharp turn and starts to drop its load. If you can find bedrock, that's even better. Orofino Creek offers some good access points, but bedrock isn't always easy to reach.

Before heading out into this area, check in with the Miner's Shanty gold-prospecting shop in Pierce. It's located in an old saloon right on Main Street; look for advertising for major prospecting suppliers. Be prepared to spend a little money on a new pan, a new snuffer bottle, some literature, etc., and trade the cost for updated information on the area. The proprietor will steer you toward some well-known locations that have been reliable in the past. Pierce Hardware is another option.

The French Creek placer operation was at 46.5310, -115.6502, and there have been GPAA claims at 46.5659, -115.6193. If you come in from Pierce, there were placers on Crystal Creek, Irish Creek, and Elk Creek, among others. I listed a spot that is above the GPAA claims in a nice meadow with great camping. Note that you can continue on this road to reach the North Fork of the Clearwater River, and there are more placer areas between you and the mouth of Orogrande Creek, which is also a great spot at 46.6310, -115.5077, about 6 miles farther north. You can reach Superior, Montana, via this route, over Hoodoo Pass; it is about 100 miles from Pierce to Superior. There are dozens more placer mines reported up on the North Fork.

30. Musselshell

See map on page 87.
Land type: Large abandoned quarry
County: Clearwater
GPS: 46.35128, -115.75872; 3,217 feet
Best season: Year-round
Land manager: USDA Forest Service–Clearwater National Forest
Material: Eocene plant fossils
Tools: Geology pick, chisels
Vehicle: Any
Accommodations: None at site; a herd of cows camps at the mouth of the quarry; developed campgrounds on nearby Lolo Creek; primitive campsites in the general area on national forest lands to the east and north
Special attractions: Northwest Passage Scenic Byway; Gold Rush Historic Byway; Clearwater River; Lewis and Clark site at Weippe

Search the big quarry at Musselshell for plant fossils. Look for the seam of gray ash on the ridge to the right.

Finding the site: From Weippe, head south on Main Street about 0.25 mile to East Pierce/Musselshell Road. Stay on Musselshell Road for about 12 miles to the national forest boundary. The quarry is 0.25 mile inside the national forest, on the right.

Rockhounding

At first glance, this is nothing but a big wall of basalt, and you might think you're not in the right spot. But look closely at the stratigraphy—the lines of flow after flow that are piled up here. Eventually you should be able to detect a distinct dark gray horizon between some rusty orange basalt flows. This gray horizon is an ash bed laid down between flows, and it's where the fossil leaves and conifer needles show up.

With your back to the road, look to your right for the fragments of gray rock that have tumbled down the quarry flanks. Search for conifer needles, probably metasequoia, and hardwood leaves such as alder.

Bring packing materials to protect these crumbly, fragile fossils. And don't over-collect—leave some for those who come after you. While most fossil collecting in the Pacific Northwest is a "search and rescue" operation, there is enough traffic through here to justify leaving material, even if it is exposed to the elements.

Keep an eye out for fish bones among the sediments. They are very rare at this locale, but you might get lucky. If you do find significant vertebrate fossils in your specimens, check in with a university or natural history museum.

If you get a chance to explore the area, be on the lookout for moose. We spotted a juvenile walking along Musselshell Road, but he quickly spooked and scrambled into the forest. There have also been Bigfoot sightings reported out here, by the way—if you have a good camera, stay vigilant.

Nearby Gold Creek is a reliable gold producer; so is Lolo Creek.

Plant fossils, including metasequoia, from the Musselshell quarry

31. Lolo Pass

See map on page 94.

Land type: Extensive diggings in alpine forest
County: Missoula, Montana
GPS: A: 46.67288, -114.60623; 6,153 feet (roadside)
     B: 46.67429, -114.60389; 6,284 feet (parking)
     C: 46.67583, -114.60213; 6,267 feet (diggings)
Best season: Mid- to late summer; snow is a challenge due to elevation.
Land manager: USDA Forest Service–Clearwater and Lolo National Forests

Smoky quartz diggings at Lolo Pass. These pits are just a short walk from the parking area.

Site 31

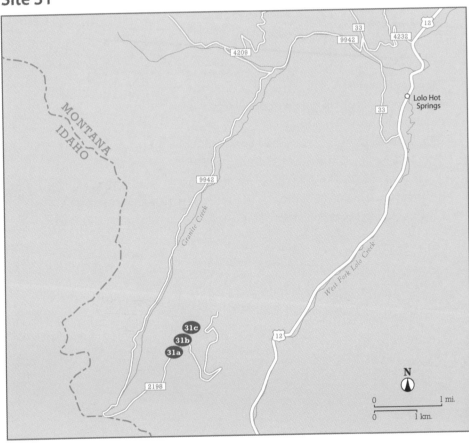

Material: Smoky quartz, pegmatite
Tools: Shovel, screen, pick, heavy hammer, chisels
Vehicle: 4WD suggested; rough roads to diggings
Accommodations: Primitive camping at site; developed sites at Lolo Hot Springs Resort
Special attractions: Northwest Passage Scenic Byway; Lolo Hot Springs
Finding the site: This site is actually just across the border in Montana, but the road you would expect to take, Granite Creek Road, is sometimes gated. Instead, head for Lolo Pass, the border between Montana and Idaho. Just at the top there is a rest area and forest service facility. About 0.1 mile past the pass to the east, look on your left for the road to Granite Pass. The signs list the distance from Lolo Pass to Granite Pass as about 6 miles, and my odometer matched that. At the pass, the main road goes down Granite Creek. Don't take that road; take the road on

the right and follow it for about 1.5 miles until you see diggings on the right side of the road that follow a small creek. This is Site A, and it is worth checking. Keep driving to the parking area at the end of the road, another 0.25 mile, to Site B. There are primitive camping spots on both sides of the parking lot. Look for a trail heading north to reach the main diggings at Site C.

Rockhounding

The diggings offer good quartz crystals in a hole right next to the road. The quartz was smoky and well-formed, with good terminations. We reluctantly pushed on and parked then walked and easily found Site C. There are extensive older diggings at Site C, and much more float material is available. Near one big boulder we found jet-black quartz fragments, plus white pegmatite float with small, dark black crystals that were elegantly formed. Use a screen to search for crystals in the dirt, or dig (or expand) a hole to bedrock and try to find crystals in place.

Not long ago a reckless gem hunter dug far too deeply, and the inevitable cave-in killed him. This sparked the authorities to threaten a shutdown. They eventually did; the status of this site is up in the air, but closed to digging as of this writing. This seems odd, as my beloved grandfather died while fly fishing, and nobody threatened to close the lake to fishing. I didn't want to leave this site out; it seemed like a good idea to offer updated information in the second edition, even if the situation isn't great. Restrict your activities to surface collecting, but be aware that the site's status is uncertain.

Most guidebooks that describe this area indicate that more pegmatite material exists throughout this section of the Idaho-Montana border. There are miles of roads worth exploring if you get the itch to discover your own private site. If you can find new logging roads, fresh culvert work, or recent road repair, you could locate a great new spot. I had poor luck along Granite Creek Road, but some reports indicate past success in the general area.

32. Lower Clearwater

See map on page 87.

Land type: Riverbanks
County: Nez Perce
GPS: A: 46.44685, -116.85956; 791 feet (Upper Hog Island)
     B: 46.47605, -116.76684; 802 feet (Potlatch River mouth)
Best season: Late fall; wait for low water.
Land manager: BLM–Cottonwood; Nez Perce Indian Reservation
Material: Sillimanite is the main prize, but there is lots of tumbler material such as jasper, quartz, and petrified wood.
Tools: Geology pick
Vehicle: Any
Accommodations: Numerous campgrounds along the Dworshak Reservoir
Special attractions: Northwest Passage Scenic Byway; Nez Perce National Historic Park; numerous historic sites around Lewiston
Finding the site: From Lewiston, head east on US 12 toward Orofino. Site A is about 10 miles east of Lewiston and is well-marked. Site B is farther out; drive 13 miles east, then turn left onto ID 3. Drive about 0.4 mile and take a right onto 285 Road/Arrow Highline Road. After you cross the small bridge over the Potlatch River, look for parking and access to the river.

Rockhounding

There was a time when it was a lot of fun to stop along the lower Clearwater and search the gravels. Rockhounds located agate, jasper, petrified wood, and the elusive sillimanite at dozens of spots. But homebuilding and development have both overtaken most of the best spots to stop, unless you can launch a kayak, canoe, or raft.

Sillimanite, also known as fibrolite, is difficult to differentiate from the ordinary quartz pebbles so common in Idaho rivers. The trick is to look for a kind of silky luster or sheen and a slight blue tint. Another trick is to look it up in guidebooks with color plates before heading out, bring home anything that remotely resembles sillimanite, and send it through the tumbler to see what emerges. Sillimanite has a hardness of 7.5 on the Mohs scale.

Basically, any spot where you can reach the Clearwater and find gravels should be interesting to search. For example, we used to stop at Arrow Beach

Wet gravels are easier to identify—another good reason to wait for low water to collect along Idaho rivers.

on the way to the garnet beds at Emerald Creek and take a long break to stretch our legs. Rounded river rock was piled up in dozens of places, but now there is development in most of this area. Ditto for Spaulding and Big Eddy. One of my older guidebooks suggests stops along US 12 at milepost 14.8, then way upriver at mileposts 74.7, 80.4, and 113.4. There are numerous sportsman access points along the river: North Lewiston, Goose Pasture, Gibbs Eddy, Mackay's Eddy, Cherry Lane, and Lenore.

Try the Mackay's Eddy access point to reach a very large gravel bar at Myrtle. You can see the gravels clearly from Google Earth. There are some BLM campgrounds along the flats, though they are busy during the summer months. Look for several small side roads along the Clearwater so you can do more exploring.

I listed the campground at Upper Hog Island as Site A because it is reliable, especially by late summer when the water is low. Another good spot is at the junction with the Potlatch River, listed as Site B. Some of the material here is from the Potlatch, which contains opal and petrified wood.

Fisher (see bibliography) shows some old fossil locales near Kendrick and Juliaetta in the giant road cuts.

33. Selway River

See map on page 99.

Land type: Riverbanks

County: Idaho

GPS: A: 46.10384, -115.56088; 1,513 feet (Johnson Bar)
   B: 46.04783, -115.29845; 1,722 feet (above falls)
   C: 46.04661, -115.29674; 1,724 feet (big bar)

Best season: Late summer for low water

Land manager: USDA Forest Service–Clearwater National Forest

Material: Quartz, petrified wood, gneiss, granite, sillimanite

Tools: Geology pick; gold pan to search for black sands

Vehicle: Any, though the gravel road gets worse the farther you drive from US 12.

Accommodations: Several developed and primitive camping areas along the Selway River on national forest lands, both above and below these sites

Special attractions: Northwest Passage Scenic Byway; Selway Falls

Finding the site: From Kooskia, drive east on US 12 for 23 miles to the junction with Selway Road, just before Lowell. Turn right and drive about 4 miles to the campground at Johnson Bar. There is parking if you're "just visiting." To reach Site B, drive about 18.5 miles, past the photogenic Selway Falls, to the first bridge above the falls. Take a left on Falls Point Road and drive only about 0.2 mile. Park safely and hop down to the gravel bar below you, visible through the trees. To reach Site C, drive 18.8 miles on Selway Road and locate the very large gravel bar below you.

Rockhounding

This can be a very pleasant journey on one of those hot August days. The cool waters of the Selway River offer a nice respite from a 90-degree scorcher. That works out well, because you need low water, late in the season, to fully expose the big gravel bars.

The hills above Selway Falls yield a constant flow of material, and the fast waters keep the rocks tumbled smooth even as far up as Site C. The rocks are clean and easy to identify for the most part. There are additional members of the basalt family, compressed volcanic ash deposits, and many common rocks in the mix here, but don't let that stop you. Thanks to the ash deposits, good petrified wood can be found here, and while the quartz isn't quite up to agate,

Sites 33–36

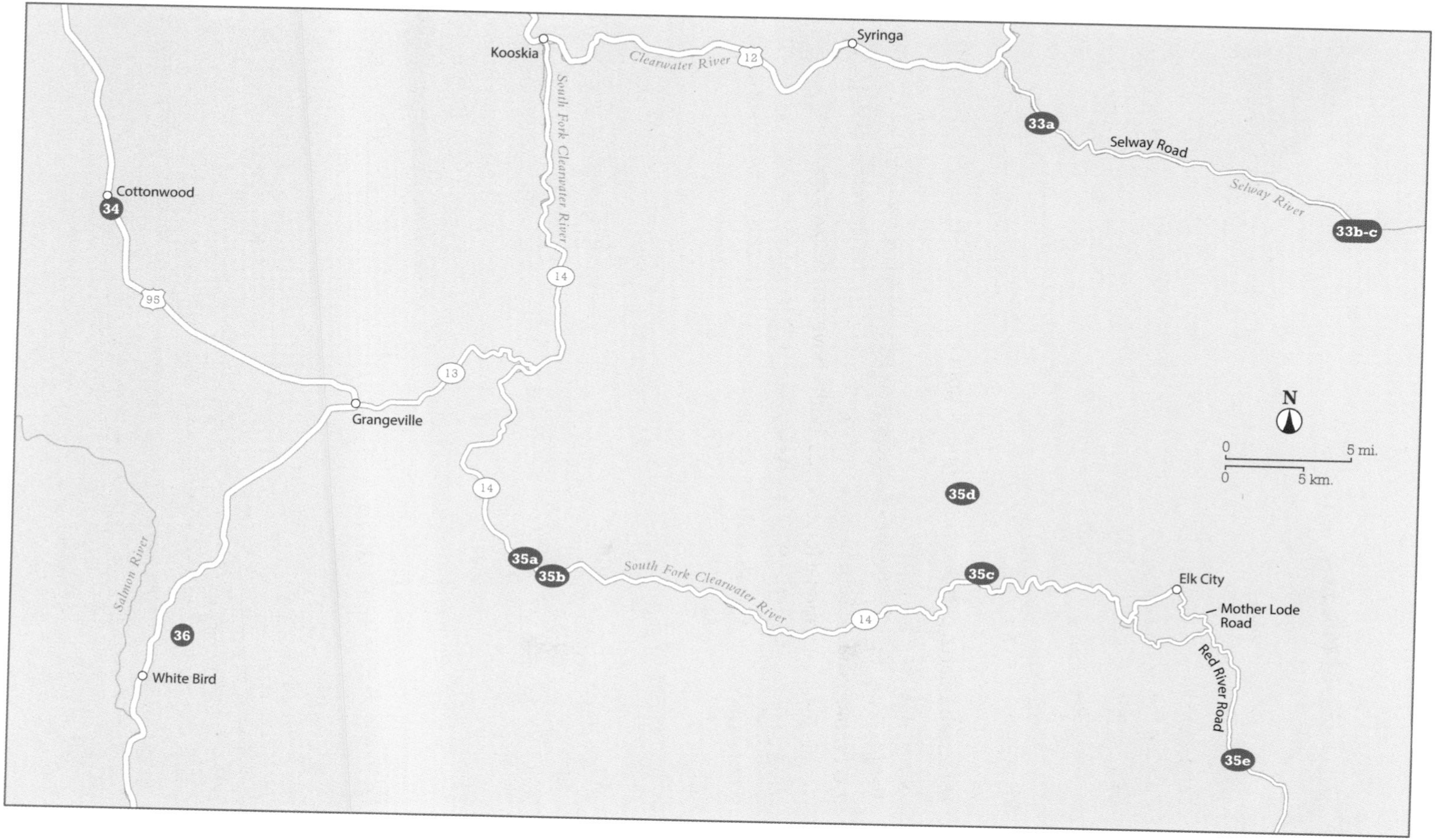

Selway River

Selway Road

33b-c

33a

Syringa

12

Clearwater River

Kooskia

South Fork Clearwater River

14

13

Grangeville

95

Cottonwood

34

White Bird

36

Salmon River

14

14

35a

35b

South Fork Clearwater River

14

35d

35c

Elk City

Mother Lode Road

Red River Road

35e

N

5 mi.

5 km.

Look for banded gneiss, jasper, quartz, and granite pebbles in the gravels of the Selway and Lochsa Rivers.

it tumbles well and has its uses. Sillimanite is reported from these gravels, but it's very rare.

There are old reports of sapphires in the gravels of the Selway and Lochsa Rivers, but I'm skeptical you could find any without opening up a hole as big as a house. Try panning a sample from a good gravity trap, such as behind a big rock or log, and see if you pull up some sparkle in your black sands. Bring a powerful hand lens so you can look closely, but don't hold your breath. Take home a big sample of concentrates and look things over in a lab or shop if possible. If you do dig a hole, please don't neglect to fill it back in.

34. Cottonwood

See map on page 99.

Land type: Basalt cliffs along highway, near town
County: Idaho
GPS: 46.04534, -116.34336; 3,496 feet
Best season: Any
Land manager: Idaho Transportation Department
Material: Small siderite spheres and botryoidal masses in basalt
Tools: Heavy hammer, stout chisels
Vehicle: Any
Accommodations: None at site; primitive camping to the east of Grangeville on national forest lands
Special attractions: Northwest Passage Scenic Byway; Tolo Lake Mammoth Site; Rice Creek Bridge across Salmon River
Finding the site: This is a very easy site to find. Cottonwood is just west along US 95. Drive to the southern end of town, where Main Street/East Road intersects US 95, and look for a large brown basalt cliff with ample parking. The cliffs stretch for about 0.2 mile.

The basalt cliffs south of Cottonwood on US 95 contain black botryoidal masses of siderite in basalt cavities.

Rockhounding

Look near the middle of the cliffs and inspect closely for round pits and voids in the basalt where a sizable "ball bearing" might have resided. The siderite, which is iron carbonate, erodes quickly from the basalt as soon as it encounters water, so you need to crack open fresh basalt to actually locate a sphere. Most of the siderite spheres are less than 0.25 inch in diameter, so adjust your goals accordingly.

I tend to find more masses of botryoidal siderite than I do actual spheres, at least in an unweathered state. Still, those can make for nice displays. Be cautious when trimming material to a manageable size—the first time I was here I broke my best specimen with one accidental blow.

There is plenty of room to park and roam here, but keep kids and pets safe. Also, my advice would be to do heavy sledgehammer work away from the cliff faces. Some of those rocks look like they are ready to let go and come crashing down.

Look for decent jasper as the cliffs peter out on the right (southeast).

35. Elk City

See map on page 99.

Land type: Forested creek beds and riverbanks

County: Idaho

GPS: A: 45.83703, -115.98871; 2,255 feet (Clearwater gravels)
B: 45.82563, -115.96187; 2,317 feet (Clearwater gravels)
C: 45.83423, -115.60233; 4,407 feet (hydraulic mine)
D: 45.88051, -115.61925; 3,913 feet (Nugget Creek mouth)
E: 45.72362, -115.37848; 4,328 feet (Gold Point Mill)

Best season: Late summer for low water

Land manager: USDA Forest Service–Nez Perce National Forest

Material: Gold and black sands; tumbler material from the Clearwater River

Tools: Gold-panning equipment, geology pick

Vehicle: Any; 4WD suggested for exploring

Accommodations: Many primitive camping spots and developed camping throughout the area on national forest lands. My favorite developed camp is Sing Lee Campground on Newsome Creek, above Site D.

Special attractions: Northwest Passage Scenic Byway; Red River Hot Springs Resort

Finding the site: From Grangeville on US 95, head east for Elk City on ID 14. Site A is about 5 miles from the intersection of Mount Idaho Grade and ID 14. Site B is another 2 miles east, toward Elk City. To reach Site C, travel about 28.5 miles from that intersection to the left (north) turn onto Newsome Creek Road/NFD 1858. After 0.25 mile look for a sharp right turn heading up the hill. At about 0.7 mile look for a faint gated road heading up to the left. Park and walk up to the old hydraulic mine.

To reach Site D, drive about 4.4 miles up Newsome Creek Road. You should see a logging road headed east, up the hill. There is a trail up Nugget Creek after another 50 yards or so. For Site E, stay on ID 14 for 38 miles from the intersection with Mount Idaho Grade. Turn onto Red River Road/22 Road, headed for Dixie. At about 12 miles look for the Gold Point Mill sign and the old buildings across the river. This is a popular spot; park carefully.

Rockhounding

The Elk City area is noted for gold, and most major streams and rivers have seen extensive dredging. Bedrock is granite of the Idaho Batholith and also gneiss, plus metamorphic rocks of the Belt Series. Quartz veins in the Elk City area run up to 20 feet in width, ranging 300 feet or more in distance. Ores are native gold, pyrite, galena, sphalerite, and tetrahedrite.

At Sites A and B, look for good access to gravel accumulations, though they do tend to move around a bit. Anywhere you spot a good gravel bar emerging from the water, search for quartz, jasper, granite, schist, gneiss, garnet, and fine gold on the upper end, where the water velocity begins to slow down.

Be sure to stop at the Gold Point Mill site, where recreational panning is encouraged.

Site C is an old hydraulic mine and easy to get to. This area is called the Tenmile District in geology literature. There are many more hydraulic mines up here, including the big Leggett Placer Mine on Leggett Creek. The practice of washing a hillside away is illegal today, but these impressive workings are testament to the hard work and determination shown by early miners.

Site D is one of my favorites; we actually hiked the length of Nugget Creek (about 2.5 miles) and found good gold throughout. Toward the bottom, look for old Chinese rock piles to the south, stacked to form the outlines of tiny apartments.

Site E is the Gold Point Mill site. It's a nice panning area, accessible and productive. If you get this far, be sure to treat yourself to a swim at the Red River Hot Springs, about 22 miles from the great old town of Elk City. They sometimes close for maintenance, so before you drive all the way up, call (208) 842-2587.

There is a lot more to explore in this area. If you have a really good vehicle, you could also drive from Old Orogrande to the Gospel Hump and Buffalo Hump areas, but there was less mining way up there.

The road through Orogrande actually connects with Dixie in about 20 miles. For the truly adventurous there is also an opportunity to drive down to the Salmon River at Mackay Bar. I haven't taken that descent, but I've been around the horn to Dixie twice, and along the way we found several old mines worth searching, with plenty of interesting quartz to break up. There are reports of telluride ore from mines out beyond Orogrande. Extensive mineralization is common northwest of Dixie, but it is way off the beaten path.

Orogrande doesn't have any services, but there are some interesting buildings to photograph. The Gnome Mill site, south of town, also has some photogenic buildings.

36. White Bird

See map on page 99.

Land type: Cliffs in old highway road cut
County: Idaho
GPS: 45.78451, -116.27134; 1,882 feet
Best season: Spring through fall
Land manager: Idaho Transportation Department
Material: Fossil leaves in thin white ash beds
Tools: Light hammer, chisels; newspaper or tissue to wrap fossils
Vehicle: Any
Accommodations: None at site; RV park at White Bird; developed and primitive camping up Slate Creek and on the Salmon River above Riggins on national forest lands
Special attractions: White Bird National Battlefield Monument walking tour is a must. Hells Canyon can be accessed from here as well.

Fossil cliffs near White Bird Battlefield, Nez Perce National Historical Park. Remember to keep the road clear of debris.

Finding the site: From Everest Street in White Bird, head north on Old US 95 about 1.7 miles to the entrance of the self-guided walking tour of famed White Bird Battlefield. This is a great stop for a family that has been cooped up in the car for way too long. One piece of advice: Don't come in the back way if you're coming from the north. Take the main highway to White Bird and then loop back. The winding, twisting stretch of Old US 95 will make even the most iron-clad stomach carsick. The fossil cliffs are about 0.3 mile farther north from the battlefield, on the left side. You can easily tell where earlier fossil hunters have looked for leaves.

Rockhounding

Use a light hammer here, with sharp chisels. Your goal is to split thin layers of rock away, revealing delicate leaves that represent a moderate broadleaf forest. This is the famed Latah Formation, middle Miocene in age; there are other significant Latah deposits in Washington, as well as near Juliaetta, Idaho. It takes very little time to accumulate enough leaves to make the trip worthwhile, and if you're determined, you can come away from here with some very nice specimens. Be sure to leave a few for the next collectors, and keep the road clean. This used to be a right-of-way for Old US 95, but the national historical park could claim the roadbed in the future and lock off this site, especially if it gets abused.

If you have time, take a run down to Pittsburg Landing from White Bird. The drive is 18 miles one way and is very steep in places—I went down there with the goals of inspecting the gold mine at the end of the lower road going north and checking a Jurassic fossil site. A pair of excellent geologists from Oregon State University assured me that neither site was worth sending readers to.

Get enough of a sample to make a nice souvenir, and then move on.

37. Slate Creek

See map on page 109.
Land type: Cliffs in old highway road cut
County: Idaho
GPS: 45.63874, -116.24715; 1,859 feet (zeolites in cliffs)
Best season: Spring through fall
Land manager: Idaho Transportation Department
Material: White zeolites
Tools: Light hammer, chisels
Vehicle: Any
Accommodations: None at site. RV park at White Bird; developed and primitive camping up Slate Creek (North Fork Campground is about 4 miles east) and on the Salmon River above Riggins on national forest lands.
Special attractions: White Bird Battlefield walking tour is a must. Hells Canyon can be accessed from here as well.
Finding the site: From US 95 south of White Bird, turn east onto Slate Creek Road. Drive about 0.3 mile, then stay left to take CR 354. Drive about 1.9 miles on CR 354 to the cliffs. Park safely. You can't miss the basalt outcrop with the spotted rock. This road takes you to USFS land after 4 miles, and Florence is about 28 miles away.

Rockhounding

This is an excellent zeolite locale, and far off the main road. The crystals are still very fresh. The needlelike material is natrolite; the crystals are analcime. Some of the veins are likely chabazite.

Zeolites are a curious mineral common in certain basalt terrains. Zeolites are often used in kitty litter to absorb odor, or in water filters. Their ringed structure attracts moisture, and some zeolites start to turn brown once they hit the air. These varieties aren't so fragile.

You can see that the basalt cliffs here are "vesicular"—they contain loads of small holes, or vesicles. The zeolite-rich solution that ran through here filled the holes. Be very cautious collecting here, and don't let any material reach the road. This locale, which extends for quite a ways along the road, was collected years ago by famed zeolite hunter Rudy Tschernich, author

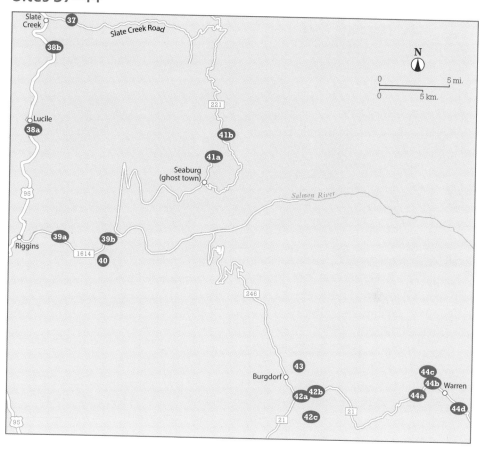

of *Zeolites of the World* and an early curator at the Rice Northwest Museum of Rocks and Minerals in Hillsboro, Oregon. There are numerous specimens in the collection and on display in the Northwest Gallery there, along with magnificent zeolites from the Challis area, covered under Site 80. Another favorite collecting site that Rudy enjoyed was at Pinehurst, farther south on US 95, but that area is no longer accessible without permission, so I took it out of this edition.

There are additional collecting opportunities along this stretch of US 95. You should be able to spot a few hydraulic mines across the Salmon River and lots of mining activity signs. There are at least two visible adits along the highway, and one is likely still for sale. If you spot a safe area where the calcite veins are especially noteworthy, stop and see if you can find the calcite in its "dogtooth" habit, where you can see the termination of multiple crystals and

Zeolite vesicles, likely analcime, in basalt along Slate Creek

they look like teeth. Also look for gold in the calcite. Be especially careful parking along the highway here.

If the Snake River is low, a couple beaches are worth checking out for agate and jasper; and if you can take a leisurely raft trip through Hells Canyon, this would give you a chance to stop at some gravel bars that don't see many rockhounds. With the Snake being a Wild and Scenic River here, you can't do much more than collect a souvenir, however, so that's why I mention it only in passing.

38. Lucile

See map on page 109.
Land type: Highway and side-road cuts
County: Idaho
GPS: A: 45.52644, -116.30337; 1,767 feet (pyrite)
  B: 45.61112, -116.27325; 1,674 feet (serpentinite, tumbler material)
Best season: Year-round
Land manager: Idaho Transportation Department
Material: Pyrite cubes, mostly altered to limonite; serpentine, zeolite; gold panning in river
Tools: Hammer, chisels
Vehicle: Any
Accommodations: Primitive camping up Slate Creek; RV parks along US 95 at Riggins. BLM offers several developed campgrounds in this area.
Special attractions: Salmon River
Finding the site: These sites are right on US 95, or very near. From Riggins, drive 8.6 miles north on US 95 and look for a combination of thinly bedded schist and a spot to start thinking about pulling over. Site A is the new rest area, which gives you access to the shale area that stretches for about 0.3 mile north.

Site B is about 15 miles north of Riggins. The road makes a giant loop around a big pit, and the green serpentinite is easy to spot in the road cut about 0.2 mile from the highway. This is actually Old US 95, and there is a small rest area near here.

Rockhounding

Site A is a rest area where you can park safely and dash across the highway to access the shale cliffs. If you have dogs or kids along, don't let them out if there's heavy traffic. Alternatively, you can park on the east side of the highway; there are some dirt roads that lead to the old highway, so it's safer.

Be cautious about rock over your head too. You should, however, be able to quickly find a few little black cubes in the slate if you make your way over to the outcrop. If you are truly lucky, you might find the brassy pyrite, but mostly I found the pyrite already altered to limonite. Still, it makes for an attractive specimen.

The thin sheets of slate and phyllite sometimes host small cubes of pyrite or limonite, altered from pyrite.

Site B has a fairly lackluster green rock, but the serpentinite is interesting. It tends to get forced upward from great depths, and is sometimes called "watermelon seed" intrusive because it forms vertical lenses and pods. The white streaks are talc mixed with asbestos, so avoid it. Down below Site B is Long Gulch, a giant pit with excellent Salmon River gravels for tumbler material. I see people camped down here all the time, although probably more for the fishing than the rockhounding.

As mentioned under Site 37, if you spot a safe area where the calcite veins are especially noteworthy, stop and see if you can find the calcite in its "dogtooth" habit, where you can see the termination of multiple crystals and they look like teeth. Also look for gold in the calcite. Just about anywhere you can reach gravels on a good inside bend, you can pan gold from the Salmon here. Blackhawk Bar at 45.62738, -116.30172 is a favorite.

39. Salmon River

See map on page 109.
Land type: Riverbank, gravel bar
County: Idaho
GPS: A: 45.41626, -116.25836; 1,725 feet (Music Bar)
  B: 45.41351, -116.18298; 1,798 feet (above bridge)
Best season: Late spring through late fall; try to time your trip for low water.
Land manager: USDA Forest Service–Nez Perce National Forest
Material: Smooth, rounded river rock, especially quartz-agate and jasper; also slate, schist, granite, and other metamorphic rocks

Massive gravel bars emerge on the Salmon River by July or August. Search for quartz, agate, jasper, gneiss, granite, and much more.

Tools: Bucket

Vehicle: Any, though stretches of the drive are rough gravel. Road construction is common in this area. Don't continue much past Ruby Rapids if you don't have a sturdy 4WD.

Accommodations: Developed and primitive camping throughout the area along the Salmon River on national forest lands

Special attractions: Riggins; Florence; lodge at Riggins Hot Springs; Burgdorf Hot Springs

Finding the site: From Riggins, drive about 3.9 miles east from US 95 on Big Salmon Road/NFD 1614 (later becomes Salmon River Road). Once you reach the mileage, look for a short access road on the left down to the gravel bar. This access road is very rough toward the bottom, so passenger cars and minivans should park early. Site B is 8.5 miles from Riggins. During road construction, I've seen this road blocked, so beware if trucks are rumbling up and down it. During low water, there are many more spots to search.

Rockhounding

As you drive up the Salmon River after leaving US 95, check out the old riverbank above you. Notice the thick sequence of rounded rock caught up in an impressive conglomerate about 0.9 mile from when you leave the highway. Do not collect here; rocks are continually falling onto the road. Instead, start looking for spots where gravel has accumulated along the river. The later the season, the lower the water, and you should find several spots to inspect.

The unnamed gravel bar I pinpointed at Site A has excellent material. My favorite method is to look in the shallows, especially where the water is just inches deep, and then walk with the sun in front of me. The agates tend to light up using this technique.

Don't restrict your search to the usual suspects—there is more than agate, jasper, and petrified wood here. Look for strange breccias that resemble carpet backing, as well as slates and schists, sometimes metamorphosed into gneiss. The granite, when clean and smooth, represents the great Idaho Batholith and takes a good polish. You should also be able to find specimen pieces from the outcrops of garnet schist up the river. If you have a gold pan and a screen, locate the head of the gravel bar and make yourself a nice sample to pan out. See if you can recognize black sands, red garnets, and faint traces of gold.

Gravels from an old gravel bar forming a loose conglomerate

There are many more gravel bars up and down the Salmon River, and if you have a decent vehicle, you can explore for miles. Site B is a popular pull-out for rafters and has a very nice beach. I hoped for better spots on the other side of the river toward Riggins, along the rough dirt track that parallels the north shore, but the only good sites come out later in the season.

40. Ruby Rapids

See map on page 109.
Land type: Riverside cliffs
County: Idaho
GPS: 45.40295, -116.19799; 1,826 feet
Best season: Spring through fall for outcrop; late summer for river panning
Land manager: USDA Forest Service–Nez Perce National Forest
Material: Garnet-bearing schist
Tools: Heavy hammer useful; screen and gold pan if water is low; hand lens
Vehicle: Any; road in is mostly paved. Construction projects can make this stretch challenging for sedans and minivans, but not impossible.
Accommodations: Multiple developed campgrounds and primitive camping areas along the Salmon River
Special attractions: Florence Mining District; Marshall Lake Mining District. Riggins is a fun and lively little town during the season, with multiple rafting operations.

These boulders are a bit precarious to scramble around, but they offer shade on a scorching day.

Finding the site: From US 95 at Riggins, take Big Salmon Road/NFD 1614 (which later becomes Salmon River Road) about 6.4 miles to the bridge across the Salmon River. Cross this bridge. If you go left, the road is unimproved and snakes back along the river toward Riggins. There are some great camping spots down that road, but it is rough. Instead, drive about 0.9 mile to the major outcrops on your left and park in the tight shoulder parking area. If you want to collect some garnet schist from the outcrops, be careful around the road, and make sure you leave it clean, even if other rockhounds or Mother Nature left some rocks on the asphalt. To reach the good garnet gravels, continue up the river on foot 0.2 mile and locate the huge boulders along the river. There is no good parking for this spot; don't be tempted to block a landowner's driveway 500 feet away.

Rockhounding

Look for large pieces of garnet-bearing schist left behind by other rockhounds, or make your own rubble and get what you need. The garnets are easier to see if you have good sunlight; bring a hand lens for closer inspection. The garnets tend to be small and brittle, but you can get intact pieces if you screen some of the dirt from below the cliff. Keep the road clear.

You can also dig up some of the dirt from the cliff face, put it into a bucket, and bring that down to the river to screen and wash. This is almost guaranteed to get some nice garnet that hasn't moved very far and should therefore be intact.

All gravels look good when polished and wet, but the Salmon River has amazing variety.

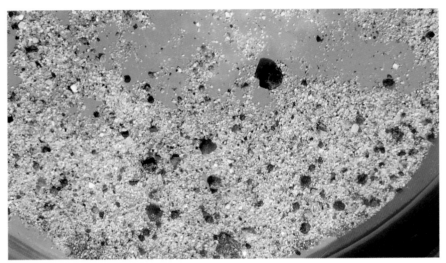
Every pan from the gravels here should yield some decent garnets.

Alternatively, you can work the gravels of the Salmon River if the water is low. The north bank of the Salmon from here up to the boulder field is very productive, although you may have to dig, and it only works if the water is low. Find any big boulder and dig around it, as this is where heavier material tends to settle. Another good spot to look for garnets (and gold) is at the top of this gravel bar, where the heavy material first settles out as the water slows down. This is classic gold prospecting, adapted to garnet hunting, as this gravel bar is just starting to form above the big boulders. It's an inside bend in the river where material has begun to pile up. Searching for these traps is a lot easier when the water is at its lowest, so try to time your visit for August or September, and pay attention to weather conditions to make sure you don't show up right after six days of rain. The big boulders also offer some shade during the hot part of the day, but they're a bit of an obstacle course and probably not suitable for small children. It's a weird feeling having tons of rock perched precariously above you, but in some places you can see a clear concentration of small garnets and black sands on the beach here.

41. Florence

See map on page 109.

Land type: Alpine forest, swamps
County: Idaho
GPS: A: 45.50221, -116.02882; 6,084 feet (town)
     B: 45.52439, -116.01322; 6,025 feet (old hydraulic pit)
Best season: Summer only; snow can cause problems into late July.
Land manager: USDA Forest Service–Nez Perce National Forest
Material: Placer and lode gold, extensive black sands
Tools: Gold pan, geology pick; heavy hammer can come in handy.

A lonely sign marks the site of the tent city of Old Florence.

Vehicle: 4WD only

Accommodations: Primitive camping throughout the Florence area on national forest lands; developed camping near Riggins and along the Salmon River

Special attractions: Salmon River

Finding the site: From Riggins, head east along the Salmon River on Big Salmon Road/NFD 1614 to the bridge, about 6.4 miles from US 95. Cross the bridge and pass the Ruby Rapids site. About 3.1 miles past the bridge, locate the road up Allison Creek; this is NFD 221. After about 12.8 miles, turn left onto NFD 394 and go about 5.7 miles. Take the left turn onto NFD 643, which is Florence Road. Good signs will guide you the final 6 miles.

You can reach Florence via Slate Creek from the north. Also, road numbers on the ground are at least thirty years old and may not match up with new printed

View south of the Salmon River from the ridge near Florence

maps and Google Earth, but the signs point you in the right direction. I found this all very confusing, so I thought it would be nice for you to know going in that the signs work. About 1 mile from the markers that designate the Florence townsite, we confronted a large tree across the road. A man in a Jeep behind us used his winch to clear a way around for himself. Be aware that these roads are infrequently maintained because it is such a remote area.

Rockhounding

This is placer gold country, so be prepared to do some digging, screening, panning, and sluicing. Try to bring home as much concentrate as you can pack out. Otherwise, you can collect quartz with rusty staining and see if the samples make your metal detector beep.

"Fabulous Florence" was one of the big early gold rushes into Idaho's backcountry. While most of the United States was engaged in fighting the Civil War in 1863, miners in Florence were finding gold at the rate of $100 per pan in the best of the earliest days. Up to 1 million ounces of gold may have been produced in this district; early records are spotty. Thousands of miners swarmed the hills, but after the early success, most of the surface deposits petered out. Lode mining never really took off up here. Frustrating snowpack choked the passes into midsummer, and water ran out way too fast for a good, long season. Still, experts conservatively estimate that more than $3 million came out of Florence, based on gold priced around $16 per ounce.

Every creek in this area yields black sand and flour gold, as long as you're near the Florence Basin. Topo maps show dozens of old prospects and placer mines in this area. Try to find old reports from Dr. Waldemar Lindgren, one of the founders of the journal *Economic Geology*. Black Sand Creek, Last Chance Gulch, and Baboon Gulch are all prominent in the early literature. Bedrock in the area is 4 to 10 feet deep and composed of decomposed granite, with quartz veins rich in gold. The challenge is dodging claim markers, which change frequently.

42. Ruby Meadows

See map on page 109.
Land type: Alpine forest, broad valleys, placer tailings
County: Idaho
GPS: A: 45.25846, -115.87792; 5,997 feet (Secesh River below mouth of Ruby Creek)
    B: 45.24881, -115.89079; 6,161 feet (lower Ruby Meadows, below hydraulic)
    C: 45.23633, -115.87711; 6,107 feet (below meadows)
Best season: Late summer for low water
Land manager: USDA Forest Service–Payette National Forest
Material: Corundum, gold, garnet, black sands
Tools: Screens, shovels, sluice box, gold pan
Vehicle: Any for Site A; foot travel for Sites B and C
Accommodations: Developed camping above Burgdorf and at the Ruby Meadows trailhead; resort cabins at Burgdorf Hot Springs; primitive camping throughout the area on national forest lands, especially along the Secesh River
Special attractions: Burgdorf Hot Springs
Finding the site: From McCall, drive north along Lake Payette following Warren Wagon Road to Burgdorf. Just before the turn to Burgdorf, which is definitely worth a visit, there is a sign for the Ruby Meadows trailhead on NFD 364. Site A is about 1.1 miles past the trailhead sign, off to the right, and offers primitive camping along the river. Otherwise, take NFD 364, which leads to the campsites then the trailhead after about 0.35 mile; you can park here and walk about 0.5 mile to the first diggings at Site B. Site C is at least 1.5 miles farther, at the northwest end of Ruby Meadows.

Rockhounding

For once, there are actually rubies in an Idaho stream with the name "Ruby." They are rare, but corundum is plentiful. To find good corundum here, be prepared to screen and wash a lot of gravel. Use multiple pans, or use a sluice and clean it out regularly. The first corundum you find will probably be small, so a hand lens can help. It is generally gray and indistinct, but some pieces will be light pink, light purple, or even ruby red; but again, actual rubies are extremely rare. Once you get an eye for the material, you'll find there is a lot here. Try to find bigger pieces with at least a couple crystal faces, but note that the material here is generally not facetable for high-grade jewelry.

Crumbling old building at Burgdorf Hot Springs

In case you were tempted to pan concentrates from Ruby Meadows at the hot springs

The gold miners who worked this area blasted out entire hillsides with hydraulic monitors, piling up gravels everywhere. The easy gold is gone, but finding black sands rich with magnetite, garnet, and corundum is still possible. The oldest rocks in this area are Precambrian schist, quartzite, and gneiss of the Belt Series. In the Cretaceous, these rocks were intruded by the Idaho

Check the gravels for corundum along the Secesh River, especially downstream from the mouth of Ruby Creek.

Batholith. The resulting quartz veins contain gold, galena, sphalerite, tetrahedrite, pyrite, and stibnite, with mica and calcite.

Site A is along the Secesh River, named by Confederate sympathizers who checked allegiance by asking if newcomers were "secesh," short for "secessionist." At Site B, lower Ruby Meadows, you can follow the miners' work down the small creek to the river. Site C is more of the same but is overgrown, and there are smaller piles surrounding the small pond. Because corundum and garnet are heavy, the miners were sometimes frustrated with the gray crystal chunks that would overload their sluice riffles. If a Hungarian riffle on a gold sluice fills up with the wrong material, it can wreck the water circulation and lose the heavies. The only recourse is to stop and clean the riffles more frequently, reducing productivity but increasing recovery. If you want a challenge, maybe hike to the top of Ruby Mountain and look for good ledges along the way. Then again, that might be as crazy as looking for diamonds along the hike to the top of nearby Diamond Rock or Diamond Ridge just to the south; it's doubtful there are diamonds up there.

Ream (2012, 114) lists another dig site at Threemile Creek near 45.30403, –115.93662, but this area is overgrown, and you may simply have to work the creek. The horse camp there gives good access.

Corundum is an aluminum oxide that ranks 9 (out of 10) on the Mohs hardness scale, surpassed only by diamond. Thus you can easily scratch a steel knife blade with corundum. If you find a reddish corundum, you have a ruby. If the corundum is blue, you have a sapphire. Most all the corundum here is a light gray, but it's still worth adding to your Gem State collection.

43. Crystal Mountain

See map on page 109.
Land type: Alpine forest, quarry
County: Idaho
GPS: 45.28938, -115.89317; 6,937 feet
Best season: Summer; high elevation can mean snow past late spring.
Land manager: USDA Forest Service–Payette National Forest
Material: Quartz
Tools: Heavy hammer
Vehicle: 4WD recommended for drive to top; steep, bumpy, and sharp turns
Accommodations: Developed site at Jeanette Campground just after the turn to Crystal Peak; dispersed camping throughout this area. Many rockhounds camp at the top in the flat area for the view; there are old fire rings all through here.
Special attractions: Burgdorf Hot Springs; Edmundsen cabin
Finding the site: From McCall, drive west along the south shore of the lake on West Lake Street, away from downtown to the turn for Warren Wagon Road. Turn north toward Warren and continue for 28.2 miles to the turn for Burgdorf Road/NFD 246. The turn to Ruby Meadows is a very short distance before your turn, but for this site head northwest 2.2 miles, past the hot springs, to the right turn for Jeanette Campground and Crystal Mountain. Drive up this steep and sometimes rutted road with numerous sharp turns for about 2.3 miles; turn into the wide flat gravel area that is essentially the top. The road loops all the way around the peak, but it's not a great road; it's much easier to just walk and scout for good specimens.

Rockhounding

Crystal Mountain has all kinds of quartz, in pastels of yellow and pink. Crystals are actually rare and occur in cavities, or vugs, which are mostly wiped out. It takes a lot of work to break out material from these cavities, and you'll see the results of that labor below the main face. You can search around the site for more vugs as well.

Historically there was a lot of mining activity in this general area. The main road to Riggins is NFD 246, and it gets exciting as you come off the mountain and get to the Salmon River. We stopped at many of the creeks and tried a few sample pans; Lake Creek had the most colors. NFD 319/Corduroy Meadows Road takes you up to the old Gilbert Placer on upper Lake Creek, around

Giant cliff of quartz at the top of the quarry

Quartz boulder from Crystal Mountain showing crystals and quartz matrix, on display at Burgdorf Hot Springs

45.37427, -115.91038. Continuing to the Salmon on NFD 246, the Edmundsen cabin is intriguing (45.37976, -116.00835). According to ultimateIdaho.com, the cabin was built in 1900. Mr. Edmundsen lived there with his family until 1930; it was a popular freight stop along the French Creek Road.

For another route to the Salmon River, come down via the old Marshall Lake mining district. I took the road from Warren to get here when I visited. There is a turn from NFD 246 just past Lake Creek that looked slow and tiring; I can't vouch for it. The Silver Summit Mine (45.40568, -115.86906) near Marshall Lake still has standing structures and interesting quartz mineralization on the dumps; there are more old mines to check, but it's a long way from civilization.

44. Warren

See map on page 109.

Land type: Alpine forest, broad valleys, placer tailings
County: Idaho
GPS: A: 45.26144, -115.71661; 5,978 feet (Halls Gulch)
    B: 45.27522, -115.69687; 5,862 feet (bridge)
    C: 45.28048, -115.70206; 5,832 feet (crossing)
    D: 45.24874, -115.65477; 6,089 feet (Charity Gulch)
Best season: Late summer for low water
Land manager: USDA Forest Service–Payette National Forest
Material: Fine gold, garnet, black sands
Tools: Screens, shovels, sluice box, gold pan

Downtown Warren

Slow down when driving through town!

Vehicle: 4WD required
Accommodations: Primitive camping throughout the area on national forest lands
Special attractions: Burgdorf Hot Springs
Finding the site: From just west of downtown McCall, turn north onto Warren Wagon Road past the lake; continue past the turn for Burgdorf, through Secesh, and onto Steamboat Creek, a total of 42.2 miles. You will see a bridge across Steamboat Creek, also a good place to stop and check, or continue to the Site A coordinates, the site of the Dreadnought Placer. Continue on Warren Wagon Road for 1.5 miles to reach the bridge over Warren Creek (Site B). You can turn left here and go through the placer tailings in Warren Meadows, about 0.5 mile, to a stream crossing (Site C). I parked here, as the water was high, but you can cross later in the summer and continue down the road another 2 miles. To reach Warren itself, from the bridge, continue on the main road about 1.3 miles. The turn for Warren Creek at Charity Gulch (Site D) is another 1.6 miles on the main road, or 2.9 miles from the bridge. This road continues on to Big Creek and also Stibnite, about 66 miles away. Be forewarned: The road to Stibnite and Cinnabar is long and tiring.

Rockhounding

Warren Creek, and particularly Warren Meadow, was an enormous gold producer in the 1860s. You can see white tailings piles over quite a distance; they are primarily decomposing granite from the Idaho Batholith. Some of my sample pans had barely any black sand but still had color, which surprised me. Usually when you pan down and the last white material all seems to wash away, there is nothing to see, but this was different. The spot on Steamboat Creek is at the foot of Halls Gulch, and there were at least three placer operations in this area. You can see extensive tailings; there are some lode mines and prospects up the road from that first bridge as you enter the district.

The bridge locale (Site B) listed here was good as well, and someone had created a small dam to run a sluice where Steamboat Creek meets Warren Creek. There is a handy access road off to the left just past the bridge. At the crossing locale (Site C), I worked my way along a bedrock outcrop and liberated a few colors.

Warren itself gets busy during the summer, especially along the airstrip, and there is a USDA Forest Service facility in town. There were no facilities that I could see when I last visited; even the old tavern/store was closed, and the only thing open was the post office. Parts of this town are quite photogenic; they may look deserted, but you cannot explore this private property. Your best bet for exploring lode mines is to head up to the coordinates for the mouth of Charity Gulch (Site D); most of the lode mines were southwest of Warren. There were multiple placers along this stretch of Warren Creek, so look for open access as well and see if the gold is more coarse than down at Warren Meadows. Turn right at the mouth of Charity Gulch and follow the tracks as far as you care to go. There is a rough 4WD road that will connect you to Warren Summit and take you past several old prospects, or you can explore Keystone and Martinace Meadows.

45. Stibnite

See map on page 131.
Land type: Riverbanks, vast open pit mine
County: Valley
GPS: A: 44.94992, -115.35219; 5,367 feet (East Fork)
    B: 44.93038, -115.33615; 6,342 feet (old building)
    C: 44.90722, -115.32692; 6,481 feet (Garnet Creek)
Best season: July through late summer
Land manager: USDA Forest Service–Boise National Forest; some private land in area
Material: Quartz with gray-black ores of tungsten and antimony; gold, jasper, granite, gneiss; tumbler material
Tools: Heavy hammer, chisels; gold pan for black sands
Vehicle: 4WD required; roads are rough, remote, steep, and narrow.
Accommodations: Primitive camping throughout area on national forest lands, especially along creeks and rivers; developed campgrounds near Yellow Pine

Main pit at Stibnite

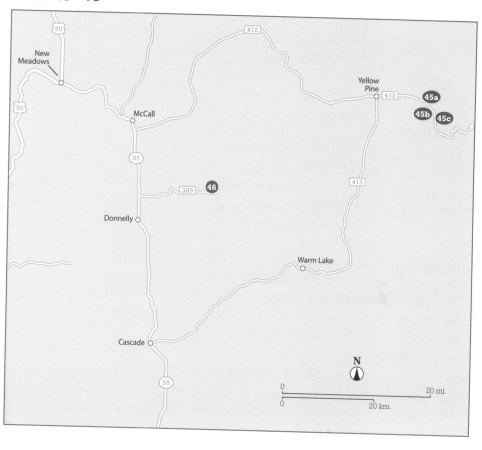

Special attractions: Salmon River Scenic Byway; Ponderosa Pine Scenic Byway; Wildlife Canyon Scenic Byway; Payette River Scenic Byway; Edwardsburg and Thunder Mountain mining camps

Finding the site: Getting to Yellow Pine is problematic. The road in from Burgdorf and Warren gets dicey in several places but is passable in late summer with the right vehicle. The road over the pass from McCall is very bumpy at the top, and not for the timid; it gets much better after that. Probably the easiest route is from Cascade via Warm Lake, then north to Yellow Pine, but that may be out of the way for you.

From Yellow Pine, head east on Stibnite Road, marked as NFD 412. Skip the turn to Big Creek about 4.4 miles out and proceed farther east. The safe parking site at Site A is about 8.8 miles past the turn. There were some massive avalanches out here recently that clogged up the creek with giant jumbles of downed pine; just about any access to the creek will provide good panning, so be flexible. If you see something that looks good before the turn to Big Creek, try it; just park safely. Continue to the rest of the sites at Stibnite. At about 11 miles from Yellow Pine, look for a rocky road that heads slightly left and down. The old building is Site B.

Site C is at about the 13.2-mile mark on NFD 412; follow the main road past the observation deck. Curve left at the intersection and go about 0.2 mile.

Rockhounding

Stibnite is named for the ore of antimony, which came out of the giant pit here as well as tungsten. The Stibnite area was a struggling gold producer until tungsten became a critical commodity during World War II. The town then flourished until about 1952. Most of the structures were still up until the late 1970s, but today most everything is gone. There is a cool observation platform at 44.92622, -115.33763.

Geology reports indicate that the oldest rocks in this area are quartzite, conglomerate, mica schist, limestone, dolomite, and tactite, of Ordovician age. These were intruded by the Idaho Batholith, with many dikes cutting through the country rock. Ore minerals include disseminated deposits of pyrite, stibnite, and scheelite. Other deposits consist of cinnabar, and start about 1 mile east of Stibnite.

For starters, try the big gravel bar on the East Fork of the South Fork of the Salmon River at Site A. Look for smooth granite, gneiss, quartz, and mica schist, plus jasper. Once you are dialed in, proceed to the big pit at the Yellow Pine Mine. Site B is located next to one of the only old buildings still standing in Stibnite. We parked there and walked the rest of the way down to the pit on the first visit, but by 2019 you could drive in to an office and announce yourself. Officials here are reasonably rockhound friendly, but they need to know why you're here, so be sure to check in. There is interesting rock everywhere; especially quartz with rusty staining that can hold the gray ores of tungsten (scheelite) and antimony (stibnite).

Site C may be near a current mining area, but the creek is far away from their activity. Search for nice quartzite and more quartz ore while you're there, but mostly this is a garnet hunt. The creek bed is dry in summer, so look for a ribbon of green and settle for digging a bucket of pay dirt you can pan later. There may be activity around the new shed; if you spot someone, check with him or her about safe specimen collecting. There are displays marking the original Stibnite townsite, but no trace remains; it was under the tailings pile 0.75 mile due southwest of Site C. If you have time, check the road that

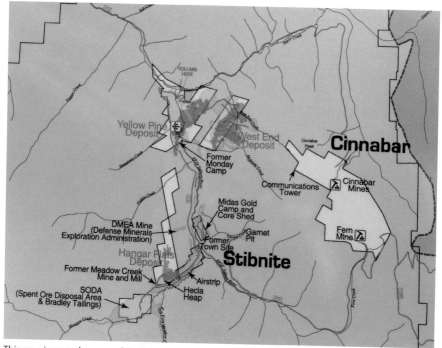

This map is posted on one of the information signs.

leads to the ghost town of Cinnabar. The other way out of Stibnite takes you to perhaps the most remote gold-mining area in Idaho, the Dewey Mine at Thunder Mountain.

There are current plans (and funding) to complete a major fish habitat rehabilitation project at Stibnite, and access could be problematic in the future, so be aware. Also, gas is available in Yellow Pine, but expensive. If it all seems too busy and you want to keep moving, try heading on up to Thunder Mountain. There are numerous prospects along the road before you reach the mines up there, and it's less active.

I once drove to the Stibnite area via ID 21 out of Idaho City, detouring through Bear Valley. The black sands on Bear Valley Creek are incredible. Dredges in this area produced loads of rare earth elements (REEs), also known as Platinum Group metals (PGMs). All the creeks in this valley are full of black sands and a little gold, but it was the black sands that recent miners prized. When you concentrate on black sands, you can be a little less cautious, because you truly are going for quantity. Once you have enough to play with, use your magnet to separate the magnetite; you should be impressed with

Classic rusty staining on quartz gives hope for metallic ore within.

how much material avoids the magnet. You would need tons of this material to interest a smelter, but it still makes for an interesting addition to your collection of Idaho materials. The Sack Creek operation recovered niobium, columbium, zirconium, and more. The Bear Valley placer also reported uranium, zirconium, and titanium. There's a good camping area at 44.42798, -115.28568 where you can sample.

46. Paddy Flat

See map on page 131.

Land type: Forested creek valley, tailings
County: Valley
GPS: 44.77720, -115.94101; 5,326 feet (creek)
Best season: Summer; low water really helps.
Land manager: USDA Forest Service–Payette National Forest
Material: Gold, black sands, topaz, amethyst (waterworn)
Tools: Screens, shovel, gold pan, sluice, hammer
Vehicle: Any
Accommodations: Developed campground at Paddy Flat; primitive camping nearby on national forest lands
Special attractions: Payette River Scenic Byway; Payette Lake; McCall
Finding the site: From McCall, drive south on ID 55 about 10.2 miles and then turn left on Paddy Flat Road. About 5.2 miles east of ID 55, there is an option for NFD 389, which leads to the ranger station and campground after about 4 miles. Since the main campground was full, I went a little less than 0.1 mile, took a left, and camped right on the creek. It looked like this was "overflow" camping, with a nice flat area and a fire pit, but no picnic table or outhouse nearby.

Rockhounding

This area is an old placer digging area, and there is ample evidence of mining along the creek here. Look for good bends where heavy material hangs up, and start making concentrates by digging a deep hole. One trick is to use a coarse screen and fill your pan with a big load, but only pan it down to about a half cup of material. Set the bigger chunks aside to check later. Slide what's left into a "concentrate pan," and keep this up until that pan is full enough to pan. At that point, use a "safety pan" (a metal pan underneath) so you don't lose anything. The black sands contain exotic metals such as tantalum, niobium, and columbium, among other elements.

The old-timers reported epidote, smoky quartz, amethyst, and even topaz from this area. Although I saw lots of tailings piles where we camped, it may be that the main workings continue here farther to the south. You'd have to run a lot of material through a sluice to get enough concentrates to search for topaz, but it is possible.

Secure camp at Paddy Flat, with dog on sentry duty

This drainage ends up in the Gold Fork of the Payette River, also worth exploring. Ream (2012, 112) shows a locale at Sloans Point beyond here with low-quality quartz crystals, garnet, and epidote.

47. Goose Creek

See map on page 138.
Land type: Alpine meadow, creek bed
County: Adams
GPS: A: 44.96994, -116.17083; 4,997 feet (creek by gate)
     B: 44.97102, -116.16421; 5,091 feet (camping area)
Best season: Late summer for lowest possible water
Land manager: USDA Forest Service–Payette National Forest
Material: Rubies, garnets, sapphires, corundum, gold, even diamonds (extremely rare)
Tools: Multiple screens, shovel, gold pan, sluice box, powerful hand lens
Vehicle: Any
Accommodations: Developed camping at Last Chance Campground on Goose Creek Park Road; primitive camping at Site B
Special attractions: Payette River Scenic Byway; Goose Lake; Brundage Reservoir
Finding the site: From ID 55 between McCall and New Meadows (on US 95), locate Brundage Road, about 6.5 miles east of New Meadows. Swing north on Brundage Road and drive 1 mile to the junction with NFD 452, then turn left and drive about 0.3 mile. Park safely and investigate the creek flowing through the meadow. This is Site A. To reach Site B, go back to Brundage Road. Just across Brundage, NFD 452 heads east. Almost immediately there is a faint track heading down the hill to the creek. There's a primitive camping area here at Site B.

Rockhounding

This is the only site in Idaho where you have even the remotest opportunity to recover a diamond in your placering. A while back, some small low-quality diamonds were recovered here, with one 19.5-carat brute receiving considerable attention. There is an active mine about 0.5 mile north of ID 55 along Brundage Road—you'll see claim signs to the east—and the old "Glory Hole" described by Beckwith (44.96368, -116.17049) is there on the left.

Back in 1995, Golconda Resources announced a drilling program on their Thorn Creek property, encountering minerals such as tourmaline, barite, fluorite, copper-gold ores, and indicator garnets. The company is no longer active there, but the BLM database still shows active claims in the area. Their number has dwindled over time; this area won't be rivaling South Africa.

Sites 46–54

Goose Creek has a wide variety of material worth close inspection.

The area known as Rock Flat appears to be private land, so I restricted my search to the USFS land north of the highway. My advice is to bring back as much concentrate as you can to a well-lit lab or garage and process your material very carefully. A powerful hand lens is a must. You will have to get down to bedrock, or find a very productive trap, to have any hope of locating the best material here. Keep an eye on that Glory Hole spot on Thorn Creek—if it ever reverts to public land, it would be a lot of fun to clean out, but it would require pumping.

Goose Creek concentrates

48. Big Creek

See map on page 138.

Land type: Creek banks
County: Valley
GPS: 44.58691, -115.87210; 4,935 feet (upper area)
Best season: Late summer, when water is low
Land manager: USDA Forest Service–Payette National Forest

Wash day on Big Creek

Material: Quartz, quartzite, tumbler material including jasper; some agate, including carnelian; quartz, zircon, black sands
Tools: Screens and gold pan if searching for black sands
Vehicle: 4WD suggested
Accommodations: Primitive camping spot
Special attractions: Payette River Scenic Byway; Cascade Reservoir
Finding the site: Drive north on ID 55 from Cascade to the Warm Lakes turnoff. Proceed about 12 miles to USFS land and look for a small road that takes off down the hill toward the creek. There are numerous creek access points along this stretch, so if someone is already camping in this spot, try a little farther up.

Rockhounding

This is another creek walk, far up Big Creek, across the USFS boundary. The water is clear and cool here, and there are numerous primitive camping spots as well as some developed campgrounds. The material is quartz, quartzite, jasper, and elusive agate, including carnelian, though I found less carnelian, which disappointed me. However, the agate is larger, so that made up for it. The black sands weren't as encouraging, but better camping and firewood made it a win. You'll need low water, so come late in summer, and spend some time walking the creek banks.

The earlier edition listed a site overtaken by development, so it's gone now. I searched for a crystals locale north of Cascade but had no luck, and I also looked for a crystals site closer to McCall near Bear Gulch. Everywhere, progress had pushed the old rockhound spots off the "active" list—but Big Creek survives.

Assorted quartz, quartzite, and red jasper

49. Mica Hill

See map on page 138.
Land type: Alpine forest, road cuts, creek bed
County: Adams
GPS: A: 44.64681, -116.39979; 3,081 feet (Middle Fork)
      B: 44.65151, -116.27009; 4,124 feet (bridge)
Best season: Spring through fall; can get blistering hot in summer
Land manager: USDA Forest Service–Payette National Forest
Material: Mica, quartz, calcite, quartzite, phyllite, garnet schist; tumbler material
Tools: Hammer, chisels, gold pan
Vehicle: 4WD suggested
Accommodations: Developed camping throughout the area; good primitive camping near White Licks Hot Springs
Special attractions: Hells Canyon Scenic Byway; Council Hot Springs; White Licks Hot Springs

Much of the material on this fork of the Weiser River will take a polish.

Finding the site: From US 95 about 5 miles south of Council, turn east onto Middle Fork Road/NFD 186. Drive about 3.2 miles and look for parking and an easy path to the Middle Fork of the Weiser River; this is Site A. About 1.3 miles farther, there is good access and primitive camping. For Site B, continue along the Middle Fork for a total of 11.3 miles from US 95. Just past the campground, locate the bridge and park safely. There are excellent gravel bars to the north.

Rockhounding

The Middle Fork of the Weiser River offers a few access points before reaching USFS land, but some are posted. You might have to get wet to reach the better gravels. I listed an easy one at Site A, but there are more. You can begin from the first coordinates to get dialed in and then search for gravels, bends in the river, and easy parking or camping. The material is mostly quartz and quartzite, with granite, phyllite, mica schist, and some jasper. I was surprised to not spot any petrified wood, but you may do better. Site B offers a reddish quartzite, plus more mica and mica schist.

At Site E, the Middle Fork of the Weiser River contains abundant mica from nearby Mica Hill, plus decent tumbler material such as this agate.

If you want to check for mica sheets, Mica Ridge is at 44.64761, –116.17851, above and to the west of Lake Cascade. The site I listed in the first edition near Site B is now blocked due to fire damage and private roads.

50. Little Weiser River

See map on page 138.
Land type: Riverbanks
County: Washington
GPS: 44.55284, -116.69328; 2,752 feet
Best season: Spring through early winter; makes a nice summer swimming hole
Land manager: Idaho Fish and Wildlife
Material: Tumbler material, including excellent agate and spectacular jasper; broken artifacts fairly common
Tools: Collecting bag, geology pick
Vehicle: SUV or better; the last mile of the road is a little bumpy and can get muddy.
Accommodations: Camping not advisable at site, as US 95 is very close and there is much private land. Developed campgrounds and primitive camping along Mann Creek.
Special attractions: Hells Canyon Scenic Byway. Council is a great little town—check out the Ace Saloon.
Finding the site: Your GPS may try to put you in the cul-de-sac off US 95 across the river from the site, so be aware that you need to come in the back way. From Cambridge, drive south on US 95 to Shoepeg Road and turn left (east), across the Weiser River. Immediately after the bridge, turn left onto Old Highway 95 so that you are going north, back toward Cambridge. Follow this road for a couple miles to the dead end and park. Walk about 0.25 mile upstream until you see the large gravel bar. During low water, there is ample gravel everywhere to search.

Rockhounding

This is an easy site to find and promises quick rewards. The agate material can run to the size of your fist, so be sure to include the concentrations of larger cobbles in your search. Look for banded agate, clear and cloudy agate, and some gorgeous yellow–orange agate-jasper material that appears to have caught the eye of early flint knappers. There are also amazing chunks of brown–tan jasper that are hard enough to cut and polish.

Set up a systematic grid and search slowly, keeping a lookout for anything notable. Walk toward the sun, and use shallow water if possible. There is ample agate here, and several of the small chips that I found bore characteristic marks

The extensive gravel bar at the mouth of the Little Weiser River contains abundant jasper, good agate, and excellent petrified wood.

of knapping. The older literature suggests that you could have good results if you search up to 4 miles away from the mouth of the Little Weiser, but there is so much private land up here, it isn't clear to me that you could actually access the river inside that zone. You might be able to float down, however, so if you have a lot of time, you might consider such an exploration. Alternatively, you could bicycle the developed trail that parallels the Weiser River for quite a ways, but again, be on the lookout for private land and don't cross any fences.

The nearby main stem of the Weiser River has excellent gravel bars all the way to Weiser during the low-water months. Again, private property and limited access could be a problem. That's the beauty of this site on the mouth of the Little Weiser: It's open, it's right on a huge productive gravel bar, and every annual flood will renew the material.

A small bottle of water to spray on the rocks will also help your search if it isn't a good day for swimming or rock-licking. Those gravel islands in the middle of the river are going to be better because they'll be hit less, especially as the summer wears on.

Material from the Little Weiser

If you live in this area and know your way around, consider getting acquainted with the folks at Hog Butte. The west base of that small mountain is said to be one source of the best material found here.

51. Cuprum

See map on page 138.

Land type: Mountain ridges, pit mine

County: Adams

GPS: A: 45.05022, -116.79005; 5,876 feet (Kleinschmidt Grade)

    B: 45.13229, -116.65176; 6,396 feet (Lockwood Saddle)

    C: 45.16931, -116.65139; 6,658 feet (Royal Peacock Mine)

Best season: Late summer

Land manager: USDA Forest Service–Payette National Forest

Material: Copper ores, especially malachite and azurite, with bornite, garnet, epidote, zeolite, calcite, quartz, chert, and other material

Tools: Hammer, chisels

Vehicle: 4WD strongly recommended; roads are rough, and it's a long way from services.

Accommodations: No developed camping way up here (try near Bear), but primitive camping throughout the area. The best spot, with water, is just past Towsley Spring.

Special attractions: Hells Canyon Scenic Byway; Kleinschmidt Grade; views of Hells Canyon at Kinney Point and Sheep Rock

Finding the site: My favorite way to get to Cuprum is via the Kleinschmidt Grade, an old ore-hauling road. Built years ago, it climbs from the Oxbow Dam area along the Snake River up to the top of the Seven Devils. Site A is a green chert locale along that road. Look for old rusted cars pushed off the grade as you climb. If you come in from Council and skip Site A, take Whitely Avenue to Main Street south, turn on Central Avenue, and stay on it as it becomes Hornet Creek Road. Follow that to North Hornet Creek Street, go north, then take the left onto Council-Cuprum Road/NFD 002. Drive 27.9 miles to Bear, then head left to stay on NFD 002 toward Cuprum. Stay on the main road for 7.2 miles, then turn right to stay on the main road and stay on it for 2.3 miles, through Cuprum. Continue as the road becomes NFD 105 for 1.2 miles, staying on the main road then turning left onto NFD 106; stay on it past the old Copper Cliff Mine (about 0.8 mile after the turn) for 4.6 miles to Lockwood Saddle (Site B). To reach Site C, drive north on NFD 106 for 2.6 miles and spot the jeep trail leading to the right just past the campground at Towsley Spring. This is NFD 493. It used to have a gate, but it's gone now. It's very

The Royal Peacock pit features abundant rock with obvious green copper staining.

rough and full of boulders, but manageable for the right vehicle and lasts about 0.8 mile to the mine. Many of you may just hike in. Your GPS may try to take you in via NFD 106, the right turn past the top of NFD 49; don't try it.

Rockhounding

The chert area along the Kleinschmidt is interesting, and there is another mine right on the grade. The best locale we found up here by far was the Royal Peacock Mine at Site C. Copper mines have always been a favorite of mine because you get an immediate visual clue as to the grade of the ore. If there's lots of green malachite around, you have pretty good ore, and if you find the rarer blue azurite, you're in luck. The Royal Peacock Mine has both, plus a crumbly brown-orange garnet, nice needles of green epidote, a

Find the green malachite first, then step up your game and find exotic material such as epidote and chrysocolla.

rainbow-hued bornite (sometimes called "peacock ore" for obvious reasons), rhombohedral calcite, and massive quartz. Small cavities offer chrysocolla as well. If not for the hike out, we would have brought some very large pieces home on our first trip. The second trip in with a Jeep was much better, but that drive is jarring.

There are a dozen mines out here, all abandoned, such as the Astoria, South Peacock, and Bluejacket Mines. The Copper Cliff Mine is now closed to collecting. There may still be active claims in this area, but this was never a major producer, and the initial enthusiasm is long gone. Check the cliffs around Site B at Lockwood Saddle to the northeast via a short trail, and there are some more prospects in the area of 45.12652, -116.64557, also to the east of Site B via NFD 106.

The historical gold-panning options aren't what they used to be, either. Old books show panning near Bear, but that's all private land now, and Placer Basin also appears to be private. This area is covered well in Wayne Sparling's book *Southern Idaho Ghost Towns* (see bibliography).

52. Mineral

See map on page 138.

Land type: Transition from sagebrush to light forest
County: Adams
GPS: 44.56859, -117.077; 3,117 feet
Best season: Late spring through early fall
Land manager: BLM–Four Rivers
Material: Gold ore, quartz, jasper, agate, ammonite fossils
Tools: Heavy hammer; chisels for fossils

Looking down at some of the ruins at Mineral. There are more ruins along the main road, just past the turn into the mines.

Caved adit at Mineral; note the April snow.

Vehicle: Sturdy rig for 60-mile round-trip from Weiser, which is mostly gravel but bumpy

Accommodations: Primitive camping at site; developed campsites on Mann Creek

Special attractions: Hells Canyon Scenic Byway; Snake River dams

Finding the site: From Weiser, drive east on CR 70 to Jonathan Road and turn right. Eventually this becomes Rock Creek Road. Follow this road up and past Hog Creek, through Henley Basin, and finally to the Snake River. Continue up the road to the right turn at Dennett Creek, about 5 miles. The road to the Mountain Man Lodge on the Snake was gated, so it was easy to make the correct turn. Drive about 2 miles up this decent road until you reach a main junction. Most of the mines are off to the left; the ghost town (three buildings) of Mineral is 0.25 mile past the junction. Note that this road that goes up and over to Fourth of July Creek and Mann Creek Road is now gated, so is not a good shortcut to US 95.

Rockhounding

Bring a hammer and a big sample bag, and prepare to bust up some rocks. Look for big quartz and calcite veins, and for rusty staining. Give the rocks a "heft test" to see which ones are noticeably heavy. Be on the lookout for green copper ore, and you might even find scarce traces of blue azurite.

There are probably two dozen prospects on this hillside and to the west, and some of the extremely short tunnels are still open. However, there isn't much in there, and I'd be remiss if I didn't remind you to stay outside in the fresh air. Search the tailings piles and rubble around the mine openings, and you should figure out quickly enough what the miners were after—highly mineralized oxidized veins.

The Jurassic ammonite fossils are a challenge. One dark shale site is right at the junction, and another is at the far end of the mine area, about 1 mile off the main road. Rare ammonites are found up here, so be persistent. Even a mold or impression will do.

Don't think of going into the old buildings—they're unsafe, and basically a tetanus shot waiting to happen if you step on an old rusty nail. Also, the risk of hantavirus is always high whenever you see mouse droppings.

Final note: We came up here once in late April, and there was still a little snow on the ground in the shady spots. A very large turkey "runs" the townsite up here, and he didn't take kindly to our staying up past dark and making noise. Every time someone laughed too loud, the turkey admonished us with a fierce gobble-gobble-gobble.

53. Fourth of July Creek

See map on page 138.
Land type: Pine forest and sagebrush hills, creek bed
County: Washington
GPS: A: 44.51186, -116.95509; 4,461 feet (petrified wood)
     B: 44.54699, -116.98923; 4,806 feet (quartz)
Best season: Late spring through late summer
Land manager: BLM–Four Rivers
Material: Massive quartz (silica); petrified wood
Tools: Heavy hammer and chisels, or just collect float.
Vehicle: 4WD suggested; last 0.5 mile is rough.
Accommodations: Primitive camping at site; developed campsites along Mann Creek
Special attractions: Hells Canyon Scenic Byway; Mann Creek Reservoir
Finding the site: From US 95 midway between Weiser and Midvale, look for the exit west to Upper Mann Creek Road. Stay left, follow the main road through the ranch, and drive past the reservoir. The intersection of Mann and Fourth of July Creeks is about 10.7 miles from the highway. This is Site A. There is a large sign, tilting to the right. You want the road to the left, toward Mineral. (Note: The road is now gated at the top.) About 3.1 miles from the sign, turn left, down the hill, toward the creek. After less than 0.25 mile, you will notice a nice little camping area along Fourth of July Creek; you should be able to see the gouged hillside across the creek. Park and follow the road up to the cut. This is Site B.

Rockhounding

Look for opalized petrified wood all along Fourth of July Creek, essentially from here down to Site A, the intersection with Mann Creek. The ridge to the east after starting up Fourth of July Creek has diggings about 500 feet above the creek, so look for that to get started. It's a beast of a climb, and you may want to just search the creek anywhere you can find access to the gravels if you're not up for the climb. The creek gravels are so full of quartz that you'll need really low water to find petrified wood along here. I liked the quartz better anyway, but be alert for both.

Note that spring can come fairly late to this area if the winter snows pile up. We tried once in late April and literally ran into a snowbank blocking the

The sign at the turn up Fourth of July Creek. Start looking for opalized wood above here.

road just above the reservoir. By early June things get easier, but the road over the top is iffy until July.

There is ample quartz float all along the road leading to the mine at Site B, as though overloaded trucks frequently slopped a little product. The best quartz is translucent and clean, but some other pieces were stained red or yellow and also looked attractive. I'm not exactly sure what you'd do with a bucket load of this stuff, and I didn't even bother trying to hack anything out of the hillside.

Large quartz boulder at Site B

While in the area, I followed Beckwith's directions and located petrified wood in the gravels of nearby Sage Creek. However, the caretaker at the Cambridge rest area later told me that the entire Sage Creek area is now private and off-limits. It's just as well, as it was a beast of a hike to get into the backcountry.

54. Weiser

See map on page 138.
Land type: Varied; sagebrush mostly
County: Washington
GPS: A: 44.28824, -117.20632; 2,200 feet (gypsum)
    B: 44.32114, -117.19493; 2,132 feet (Snake quarry)
    C: 44.32028, -117.07083; 2,408 feet (Hog Creek)
    D: 44.24657, -116.71311; 3,261 feet (Idaho Almaden Mine)
    E: 44.35907, -116.53557; 3,305 feet (Crane Creek)
Best season: Spring through fall are best, but avoid summer heat.
Land manager: BLM–Four Rivers
Material: Gypsum and copper minerals along the Snake; agate nodules at Hog Creek; cinnabar and pyrite at the Idaho Almaden Mine; jasper along Crane Creek
Tools: Hammer and chisels at Sites A and D; geology pick elsewhere
Vehicle: 4WD helps on gravel roads when washboards get bad.
Accommodations: Developed camping on Mann Creek; primitive camping throughout the area on BLM and national forest lands
Special attractions: Payette River Scenic Byway; Hells Canyon Scenic Byway; National Oldtime Fiddlers' Contest and Festival, held annually in Weiser
Finding the site: These locales are scattered around Weiser. To reach Site A from "downtown" Weiser on State Street, head west on Pioneer Road. Go 1.6 miles and turn right onto CR 70. Continue 4.2 miles west and turn right at Eaton Road. Go about 1 mile and turn left onto Olds Ferry Road. After about 8.1 miles, the dunes start. Look for a small dirt road headed off to the right. Park and search the cliffs to the right for gypsum crystals.

To reach Site B, continue on Olds Ferry Road another 2.5 miles and look for the quarry on the right. For Site C, turn right from ID 70, about 2.7 miles after the turn from Pioneer Road as if you were going to Mineral (Site 52). After about 2 miles, this road swings westerly and becomes Henley Basin/Rock Creek Road; stay on this main road. My reading is 4 miles from CR 70, but we started noticing material at about 2.5 miles, and there were varying concentrations along the road until at least 6 miles from the highway. This site is mostly to interest you in the Hog Creek area, however.

Idaho Almaden Mine at Site C, with good specimens in the rubble around the bottom of the cut

To reach Site D, head south from Weiser on US 95 about 1.2 miles, then swing onto Couper Road going east. After about 0.7 mile, turn right onto Day Road, then almost immediately turn left onto Cove Road/Hill Road. After about 10.3 miles, turn left (north) onto Crane/Crane Creek Road. Stay on Crane for about 4 miles, and notice the big cut that is the Idaho Almaden Mine on the right. Site E is at an intersection about 14.5 miles farther north on Crane Creek Road from Site D. Craig Road heads west here to the Crane Creek Reservoir.

Rockhounding

Site A offers an unusual chance to recover gypsum crystals, and they're easy to spot because they're falling right out of the hillside. The crystals sit in seams and chunks of rock. Site B is an abandoned quarry with copper minerals, mostly malachite, and some pyrite. Look for green streaks, and break up material here with a big hammer. I think the copper is better on the west side of the Snake River, in Oregon.

Gypsum crystals along the Snake River at Site A

Site C is not the famed Hog Creek locale, which is claimed by the Idaho Gem Club and behind a locked gate. But there are plenty of agate and jasper nodules along the road, and this is easy hunting. The old Beacon Hill nodule area is claimed by the club and alone worth joining for. If it shows up on the annual field trip schedule, be sure to get your name on the list and make the trip. You could probably find good material in the hills away from their claim, but I haven't been down there.

Site D is a famed quarry, with red cinnabar streaks and occasional pyrite; be prepared to break up rock here. Site E is another easy search—just hunt along the road and throughout the sagebrush. The red jasper here was not hard to locate.

55. Idaho City

See map on page 158.
Land type: Creek beds, tailings piles
County: Boise
GPS: A: 43.72634, -115.95292; 3,318 feet (Grimes Creek)
　　　B: 43.83188, -115.79077; 4,022 feet (recreation area)
Best season: Late summer; low water is vital.
Land manager: USDA Forest Service–Boise National Forest
Material: Gold, black sands, garnet, white quartz; tumbler material
Tools: Gold pan, sluice, shovels, screens
Vehicle: Any; 4WD suggested if you explore up at Centerville and Placerville
Accommodations: Developed campground at Grayback Gulch, off ID 21 south of Idaho City; primitive camping throughout area, especially along Grimes Creek
Special attractions: Ponderosa Pine Scenic Byway. Idaho City is a must-see—start with the tourist bureau office.
Finding the site: From Boise, head east on I-84 to the ID 21/Idaho City exit. Drive past Lucky Peak Dam, and after about 24 miles you'll see the junction of Grimes and Mores Creeks. This is Site A. There are primitive camping sites throughout this area, but they are popular with Boise campers, especially on three-day weekends. Site B is the recreation area north of Idaho City, about 36 miles on ID 21 from the junction with I-84. Turn right onto NFD 327/Rabbit Creek Road; pull into the parking area and find a nice, quiet spot to set up.

Rockhounding

The Boise Basin has produced at least 2.3 million ounces of gold so far, easily making it the most productive gold-mining district in Idaho. Several gravel bars between the reservoir and Site A offer panning access, but be sure to watch out for parking issues and private land if you try one. The GPAA has a claim 2.5 miles farther up Grimes Creek, for example, and there are more access points all the way from here to New Centerville, though there are more claims too.

Site A is reliable because both Mores and Grimes Creeks contain good gold. We camped for a weekend on Grimes Creek and kept enlarging a hole right at the spot on a gravel bar where the heavies drop out as the creek bends.

Sites 55–56

Be sure to drop in at the excellent Boise Basin Museum when in Idaho City.

Each successive piece of gold we recovered was bigger than the last, so we kept working.

Site B is a large, open area with ATVs, motorcycles, anglers, and gold panners all competing for good spots. I found some nice quartz in the tailings piles, and one beeped for my detector. I busted it up with a hammer and liberated a string of fine gold and black sand in the bottom of the pan.

Old reports for the Idaho City area can really spur your imagination. There are leaf fossils along Thorn Creek, on the south side of Placer Creek about halfway to the old campground there. The locale has been hammered, and all I found were fragments. The drive is nice, and there are good camping spots along the creek, plus modest gold and black sands.

The mine dumps around Idaho City still yield garnet and quartz, and there are reports of thin films of precious opal in the sandstones along Mores Creek. The old mines at Centerville supposedly have interesting tailings piles, but there is so much private land up there, I can't vouch for any open tailings piles you might explore. I've been here four times, and I can't seem to get out of the placer camps. I can, however, vouch for the food at Diamond Lil's, plus their collection of old paper money. Because conditions change constantly here, drop in on the helpful folks at the tourist center

Prepping a dredge to place on Grimes Creek

in Idaho City and ask questions. Plan to purchase some mining supplies in town if possible, and ask about conditions before you do much more than scratch around up here.

On the drive up, there are some interesting veins in the road cuts. At Lucky Peak Dam there are zeolite showings in the basalt cliffs near the Barclay Bay Picnic Area. The road to Atlanta is long and interesting, and Atlanta was a significant gold producer back in the day. There is another interesting museum at Placerville. The road over the pass to the Payette River is a little rough for passenger cars.

56. Dismal Swamp

See map on page 158.

Land type: Diggings in alpine creeks and marshes; granite outcrops

County: Elmore

GPS: A: 43.72205, -115.36845; 6,946 feet (granite)

B: 43.72691, -115.37272; 6,709 feet (middle; creek)

C: 43.72974, -115.36711; ,6645 feet (swamp)

Best season: July and August

Land manager: USDA Forest Service–Boise National Forest

Material: Smoky quartz, topaz (rare)

Tools: Heavy hammer, gads, chisels, screen

Vehicle: 4WD only; roads are very rough out here.

Accommodations: Primitive camping at site; developed campgrounds at Trinity Lakes

Special attractions: Ponderosa Pine Scenic Byway; Rocky Bar and Atlanta Mining Districts

Finding the site: From I-84, get off at ID 21 east of Boise and drive about 16 miles to the turnoff to Middle Fork Road, which reaches Atlanta. Follow this poor road 68 miles to just before Atlanta, then turn right and take James Creek Road south to Rocky Bar, about 10 miles south and too steep for trailers. You can also take I-84 to Mountain Home, exit onto US 20 toward Fairfield, then swing up Sun Valley Highway/US 20 about 32 miles to NFD 61/Louse Creek Road. Turn left on NFD 61 and go about 33 miles to Featherville. At the north end of Featherville, turn left onto Rocky Bar Road. Go 3.2 miles to Rocky Bar. However you reach Rocky Bar, go 6.3 miles northwest on Phifer Creek Road/Trinity Mountain Road/ Trinity Ridge Road, where you'll meet the junction with NFD 129. Phifer Creek Road/NFD 156 is a possible shortcut north to the Middle Fork Road; I've never taken it, but I saw the sign. At this junction, stay left, headed west on NFD 129/ Trinity Mountain/Trinity Ridge Road, and go 1.9 miles. Track the mileage carefully so that you see a primitive road headed right, sharply down the hill to Dismal Swamp. It's not marked. Site A is about 0.5 mile from the main road; Site B is 0.5 mile farther, and C another 0.5 mile farther down. You'll have to walk to reach the swamp at Site C.

Cool forest setting at Dismal Swamp, but full of biting flies

Rockhounding

There are three modes of attack here: (1) Walk and walk and walk, searching for crystals that other rockhounds missed; (2) increase the size of a current pit along the creek and screen material, making sure to wash big rocks before dismissing them outright; or (3) use a heavy hammer and chisels to search for vugs in the surrounding granite. I tried mode 1 and did OK, while a friend, Jason Estes, tried mode 3. He found the most amazing pieces in a dirt-filled vug, so keep that in mind.

Old photos of rockhounds working this area at least thirty years ago show lots of bare earth, aggressively worked down to bedrock in places. Today the area is covered with scrub brush that makes work far more

Jet-black smoky quartz from Dismal Swamp PHOTO COURTESY OF JASON ESTES

difficult. There were also new claims in the area to negotiate, but out of curiosity I opened up the box at the marker and the notices were dated 2004. I checked with the BLM's LR2000 database, and none of those claims were active as of 2009.

In early 2008 the USDA Forest Service was mulling over the idea of shutting down Dismal Swamp, citing concerns about fish habitat. After hundreds of complaints poured in, the planner transferred to another jurisdiction and the idea was shelved. It may rear its head again, which would be a shame. Very few people get up here anymore, and the earth healed most of the damage done by previous generations. Dismal Swamp has yielded amazing specimens in the past, including topaz up to 100 carats in weight, and the smoky quartz is also world-class. The drive up can be a bit grueling, and horseflies swarm the area, but it is worth it. Bring bug spray and wear long sleeves.

Note: During mid-July each year, Phifer Creek Road is blocked off so that the county can host a road rally. We had to wait a couple hours to get out.

57. Graveyard Point

See map on page 165.

Land type: Sagebrush desert

County: A: Owyhee; B–E: Malheur, Oregon

GPS: A: 43.57421, -117.02153; 2,498 feet (monument)
　　　B: 43.55316, -117.04789; 2,663 feet (along road)
　　　C: 43.54787, -117.05253; 2,690 feet (ridge)
　　　D: 43.54380, -117.05500; 2,811 feet (pits)
　　　E: 43.54009, -117.05106; 2,813 feet (ridgetop)

Best season: Spring through late fall

Land manager: BLM–Owyhee

Material: Plume and brown to clear agate

Tools: Geology pick for prying

Vehicle: Any for Site A; 4WD suggested for Sites B–E, but I've seen trailers in here.

Accommodations: Snake River RV Park, Homedale; primitive camping on BLM lands in the vicinity, but avoid private land, current claims, and other annoyances.

Special attractions: Owyhee Uplands Back Country Byway; Western Heritage Historic Byway; Jump Creek waterfall

Finding the site: From where the highway crosses the Snake River at Homedale, drive south 3.2 miles on US 95 to Graveyard Point Road, heading right (west). After about 3.9 miles, there is an intersection with Sage Road. Those who have been here before can turn onto Sage Road and head for the bridge across the canal. If this is your first visit to the area, drive straight through and go 0.6 mile, the last stretch up a fairly steep hill, to the canal. Stay right when two roads parallel so that you don't end up in somebody's driveway. The big Graveyard Point stone monument is to your right, and everyone should see it at least once.

　　The road will curl around to the right, but it ends with private property; older guidebooks showed a footbridge (still standing) and a vehicle bridge (private property). Instead, from the monument, head left and follow the canal to the vehicle bridge and cross over. One of the main roads will bend to the right and lead you under the power line after about 0.75 mile. The dirt road is horrible here—bumpy and rocky, and that's when it's dry. When it rains, the dust turns to gumbo and you can slide right off the track. Drive about 2.1 miles, staying more or less left, but follow the main tracks. If you end up too far right and back at the

Sites 57–66

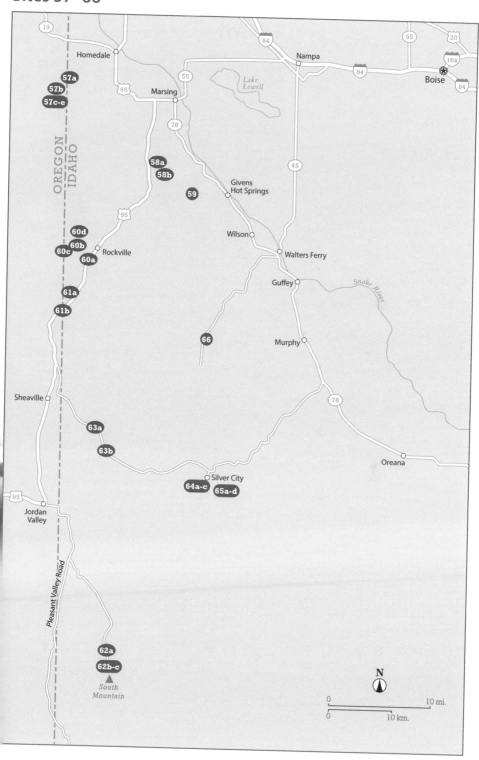

Roam the hills, walk the roads, and get to know the area.

canal, you lost the track, which isn't hard to do, as ATVs tend to obliterate the road during one stretch. You are looking for a crossroads that marks the beginning of a gentle 1-mile loop around various diggings, old workings, and claims. Work your way south, check along the road, and have fun exploring.

Rockhounding

I always end up surface collecting here, as there is so much material just lying on the dumps or out in the sagebrush. Some areas are particularly rich, and you might see the small chips that are evidence of old arrowhead workings. Bring your geology pick and pry up anything that looks remotely interesting. We found a nice plume agate the size of a softball just by prying away at a small, dime-size chunk that stuck out of the ground.

The material here is widespread, and you should leave time for a lengthy search. At Site A, the hills above the canal are excellent, and near the road is still productive. But this is the hardest hit area, so try to keep moving. This is the beginner's spot for Graveyard Point, but it's worth checking if you don't have a sturdy vehicle. Site A is still within Idaho; all the other readings are actually in Oregon.

Site B is along the road after you reach the general area. There are diggings off to the right and above you. Look for impressive float around these pits, and be ready to pry up anything that looks interesting.

Site C is farther along the road, off to the right again. My favorite way to work the loop is to stay right and then circle back to the left. This road is not suitable for any passenger car; you need high clearance and good tires. Nice bubbly agate and more plume agate can be found here.

Site D is in the middle of some impressive pits that haven't been worked in quite some time. There is surface material all over the place.

Site E is at the top of a small mountain that looks back east into Idaho. Considerable material can be found on the ground up here.

The agate collecting area here is quite extensive, and you can take any road and inspect along it or across the hills and ridges. There is primitive camping at 43.54223, -117.05254 by the old Purple Sage workings.

Assorted fist-size agate collected across the hillsides

58. Sommer Camp Road

See map on page 165.

Land type: Open sagebrush and hill country
County: Owyhee
GPS: A: 43.45824, -116.84574; 2,865 feet (jasper, queenstone along road)
  B: 43.44516, -116.83076; 2,567 feet (camp)
Best season: Spring through fall
Land manager: BLM–Owyhee
Material: Jasper, opal, and agate at Site A. Site B is near the famed queenstone deposit claimed by the Idaho Gem Club.
Tools: Heavy hammer, geology pick
Vehicle: Any, though 4WD preferable to avoid long walks
Accommodations: Snake River RV Park, Homedale; developed camping at Givens Hot Springs; primitive camping on open BLM land throughout this area
Special attractions: Owyhee Uplands Back Country Byway; Western Heritage Historic Byway; Givens Hot Springs
Finding the site: From US 95 headed south from Homedale, continue almost to Marsing. US 95 swings abruptly south before heading into Marsing. Follow the highway and drive about 5.6 miles to the big truck scales, which are brightly lit at night. Turn left onto Sommer Camp Road, which is well marked. To reach Site A, drive about 1 mile and look for the jog in the fence on the right. For Site B, continue on Sommer Camp Road a total of 2.3 miles from US 95, and look for a turnoff on the right. The road heads around and up; you can spot the creek crossing. Use this as a base camp, and check out as many of the roads as you can for good material.

Rockhounding

The Idaho Gem Club hosts an annual field trip to their queenstone claim, and I'd encourage anyone interested in western Idaho rockhounding to join them. It may be the only way to access famed sites such as the Wangdoodle opal or Beacon Hill agate nodules, for example. If you're in the area but not a member yet, try Site A and explore around Site B.

Site A is along Sommer Camp Road, but it's been picked over and you'll need to get a lot farther from the road to do much good. It's OK to cross the fence here; it is still public land. Opal and jasper are fairly common in this area,

You can slip past this fence to inspect the material farther from the road at Site A.

and if you don't have time to drive into the hills, give this location a try. The queenstone has a striking pastel appearance you will immediately recognize.

Site C is a reliable opal dig that you can spot from the road. The white diggings stand out easily from the dry, brown sagebrush. There is abundant material all over the ground in this area, but dedicated rockhounds have used picks and pry bars to remove excellent samples. The opal is generally white, sometimes with red streaks, and occasionally displays an oolitic texture.

This appears to be a mix of queenstone and zeolites; we called it "The Squid Eye." PHOTO COURTESY OF MARTIN SCHIPPERS AT KLEURCOLOR.COM

59. Opalene Gulch

See map on page 165.
Land type: Sagebrush, rolling hills
County: Owyhee
GPS: 43.41662, -116.77591; 2,615 feet
Best season: Spring and late fall; avoid wet season and summer heat.
Land manager: BLM–Owyhee
Material: Opal
Tools: Hammer, chisels
Vehicle: 4WD suggested
Accommodations: Snake River RV Park, Homedale; developed camping at Givens Hot Springs; primitive camping on BLM lands throughout this area

Opalene Gulch diggings are hot and dry, so come prepared.

Thin slice of opal in matrix

Special attractions: Owyhee Uplands Back Country Byway; Western Heritage Historic Byway; Snake River; Givens Hot Springs

Finding the site: From US 95, turn left onto Sommer Camp Road and go about 3 miles to where it intersects Clark Road. (Alternatively, coming from the east, follow ID 78 to about 5.5 miles south of Marsing, then turn left onto Clark Road, also known as Rats Nest Road). At the intersection of Sommer Camp and Clark Roads, turn right and follow Clark Road for about 3.5 miles to a right turn onto a primitive, unmarked road; continue about 0.5 mile. You can't miss the large white mounds; they're visible from Google Earth.

Rockhounding

Check for float along dirt tracks and throughout the hills, then look for pits where previous rockhounds have dug for solid opal. The material here is mostly white, but there are reports of precious opal here, and it's worth a try. As I drove in, I found a nice spot over on the right where the opal material formed in small bubbles. Several pits showed evidence of recent digging, and from all appearances it looked like good material was being found.

I found more solid pieces just walking around at random. With opal, you need to know what you like in order to effectively collect at a site. You can find larger, cuttable material or small gemmy samples of possible interest for jewelry. For the most part, Opalene Gulch material found at the surface is soft and white, with harder material found in seams in the matrix.

Fisher (see bibliography) shows another opal locale a little farther east at Hardtrigger, and there are undoubtedly more opal deposits around these hills.

60. McBride Creek

See map on page 165.

Land type: Sagebrush, rolling hills, creek beds (sometimes dry)

County: Owyhee

GPS: A: 43.32150, -116.97719; 4,285 feet (McBride Creek fossils)

B: 43.33603, -117.02265; 3,869 feet (McBride Creek float)

C: 43.34163, -117.00221; 3,947 feet (McBride Creek crossing)

D: 43.35589, -116.99805; 4,074 feet (McBride Creek side road)

Best season: Spring through late fall

Land manager: BLM–Owyhee

Material: Petrified wood, agate, jasper, opal, leaf fossils

Tools: Geology pick; chisels for removing fossils

Vehicle: Any, but 4WD suggested

Accommodations: Primitive camping on BLM lands throughout this area. Snake Valley RV Park in Marsing is a popular headquarters for those with trailers and RVs.

Special attractions: Owyhee Uplands Back Country Byway; Succor Creek in Oregon

Finding the site: To reach Site A, drive 19.1 miles south on US 95, or backtrack 4.8 miles north from the Oregon border and take a turn west onto McBride Creek Road. At about 0.7 mile, look for a faint track leading to the right. Drive down this track, park, and walk across McBride Creek to the big white cliffs.

For Site B, take McBride Creek Road 2.5 miles from US 95 until you come to a fork. The main road leads left, while a decent track heads to the right. There is more agate, opal, and petrified wood in the hills here, but the road on the right is sometimes closed in early spring to keep the four-wheelers away. If this road is closed, take the main road on the left 1.1 miles until it crosses McBride Creek, just before reaching the Oregon border. Site D is an extensive wash with excellent material in both directions.

Site C is the McBride Creek crossing, closed to vehicles in early spring but easily accessible by foot. Leave time in your schedule to follow the creek north and west, where it is joined by another creek with good gravels. Site D is about 1.1 miles north from Site B, where a small road comes in from the west.

Hardened ash spires near the fossil locale at Site A

Rockhounding

Site A is the noted McBride Creek leaf fossil area, but I always find excellent agate on McBride Creek and get frustrated with the fossils. From the parking area, keep a sharp eye out for gravel accumulations as you cross McBride Creek. The fossils are in a distinctive darker gray layer in the white chalk cliffs. There is also some low-quality petrified wood here, running to large sizes but hardly worth taking home.

Site B is the last McBride Creek locale as you leave Idaho. Search the wash in both directions for agate, jasper, and petrified wood. Some of the sharp pieces of jasper that I found in this creek look like they had been knapped.

Site C is an easy crossing for McBride Creek. If you can time your visit for soon after the spring runoff, you should do well. Agate and jasper are excellent in this spot.

Site D requires walking or driving the faint road leading west and up the hill then combing the hillside for the usual suspects: agate, jasper, and petrified

Fossil plant material recovered from a thin strip in the white chalk cliffs at McBride Creek

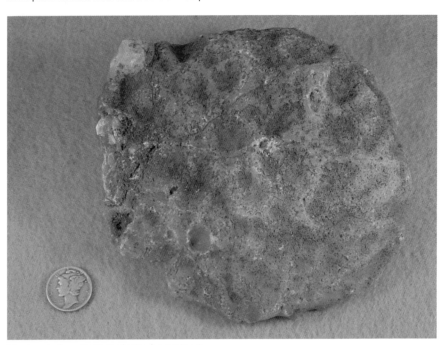

Giant agate found in McBride Creek near Site A

wood. To circle back to US 95, take the solid gravel road leading east about 1 mile from this point. The road will cross a wide wash with more excellent material.

61. Coal Mine Basin

See map on page 165.
Land type: Sagebrush, rolling hills, creek beds (sometimes dry)
County: Owyhee
GPS: A: 43.24671, -117.02585; 4,185 feet (Coal Mine Basin)
　　　 B: 43.27657, -117.01245; 4,089 feet (quarry on Texas Basin Road)
Best season: Spring through late fall
Land manager: BLM–Owyhee
Material: Petrified wood, agate, jasper, opal, leaf fossils
Tools: Geology pick; chisels for removing fossils
Vehicle: Any, but 4WD suggested
Accommodations: Primitive camping on BLM lands throughout this area. Snake Valley RV Park in Marsing is a popular headquarters for those with trailers and RVs.
Special attractions: Owyhee Uplands Back Country Byway; Succor Creek in Oregon
Finding the site: Drive south 24 miles from Marsing, or from the Oregon border heading north on US 95. At the spot where the pavement changes, take the first

Pits at the top of the road near Site A

right (the turn is about 100 yards from the border, headed east). Drive on this road about 0.4 mile, then stay left, leaving Coal Mine Basin Road. About 0.9 mile, up the steep hill, you finally come to a pit area. This is Site A, Coal Mine Basin Road. Park here and walk around, noting the pits and also the dug-up area on the hillside to the west. You can roam these hills quite a bit, and they should be productive. Continue about 1.4 miles to possibly find more source material in the cliffs starting at 43.22431, -117.01661 and working west.

To reach Site B, drive about 0.9 mile north on US 95 from the state line to the intersection with Texas Basin Road. Turn left (north) onto the dirt road and drive about 0.6 mile to the Y; bear right and continue 0.7 mile to the new quarry.

Rockhounding

Site A at Coal Mine Basin offers petrified wood, agate, and jasper in varying sizes. Some of the material is float from the hillsides, and some is concentrated in the road gravel and in the small streambed. The agate can be particularly colorful. The small knobs highlighting the skyline appear to be one source for the petrified wood, so if you have the time, hike around. We did very well along the road in a short amount of time.

Site B is on Texas Basin Road. The wash to the west is excellent, with plenty of material to choose from, but try to get to Site B and check out the new quarry. There are fossils in these rocks, although fragmented. You can also drive on the other side of US 95, which is Texas Basin. Go to the big gate about 1 mile from the highway, where you can park and search the hills and gulches. West of the highway there are reports of picture jasper and thundereggs, most likely in the white ash beds.

Fossil plant material recovered from a thin strip in the white chalk cliffs at McBride Creek

62. South Mountain

See map on page 165.

Land type: Sagebrush, alpine forest
County: Owyhee
GPS: A: 42.77176, -116.92693; 5,972 feet (marble)
  B: 42.74528, -116.92160; 6,826 feet (mine)
  C: 42.74496, -116.92048; 6,961 feet (road spoils)
Best season: Late summer
Land manager: BLM–Owyhee; some private land
Material: Ilvaite, hedenbergite, quartz, gold ore, marble, pyrite, garnet
Tools: Heavy hammer
Vehicle: 4WD recommended; rough, steep road closer to top of South Mountain
Accommodations: Primitive camping on public lands near the top of the mountain
Special attractions: Owyhee Uplands Back Country Byway; view from the top of South Mountain
Finding the site: From Jordan Valley, Oregon, head east on Main Street toward Yturri Boulevard. Turn right onto Yturri and drive 3.9 miles, where it becomes Pleasant Valley Road. Continue another 3.5 miles, then turn left onto South Mountain Road. Drive 11.6 miles and look for a road coming in from the right, which leads to the quarry at Site A. To reach Site B, drive up the mountain another 2.1 miles, past the decaying buildings at the cow camp and reach the mine. The end of the good mine spoils is another 0.1 mile up the mountain.

Rockhounding

This site, a longtime favorite for Idaho collectors, is listed in all major guides to date. We saw some rehabilitation work either going on or recently completed in 2008, and by 2019 there had been some major changes. The best news was that the miners had dumped tons of mine spoils along the road, so collecting is as easy as parking safely and checking out the material along the road. Note that all mine shacks and buildings are posted against entry. Restrict yourself to the tailings piles, and avoid putting the locale at risk.

Site A has some decent marble, appearing light gray when fresh. Hike up the short trail to the marble face and check it out. This material is a solid white and will tumble and polish well. Grab some marble if you want, but by all means, press on. The main goals here at Site C are two rare minerals: ilvaite

The large tailings pile along the road at Site C

and hedenbergite. Ilvaite is present as small, black stubby crystals, with collectors cleaning out most of the better material long ago. Hedenbergite is black to greenish, with sprays of slightly longer crystals more common. Ilvaite is usually a little blacker and stubbier. This is one of the few places in the world where you can find these two rare crystals, and they are practically mandatory for any complete collection of Idaho minerals.

Try the dumps along the road, and be prepared to break up material. If anyone is working at the mine, they might answer a couple questions for you, but most likely the active pits will be off-limits. We kept going up, and at the sharp turn we hammered on a white vein and came away with decent material; the dumps weren't as productive, as can be expected. Continue on up the road to the old lookout site, and find the spot where more vein material piled up. To get a good idea of what the crystals look like before you head out, consult mindat.org, Wikipedia, or your minerals handbook.

Dark black blades of ilvaite

63. Cow Creek

See map on page 165.
Land type: Rolling sagebrush, dry creek beds
County: Owyhee
GPS: A. 43.08479, -116.95953; 4,808 feet (wash)
B: 43.05148, -116.93362; 5,000 feet (boulders)
Best season: Spring through fall
Land manager: BLM–Owyhee
Material: Agate, jasper, opal, petrified wood
Tools: Geology pick
Vehicle: Any, if careful; 4WD suggested, especially for exploring
Accommodations: Developed campground at Silver City; primitive camping spots on public lands throughout the area

Spring can bring a lot of water to the desert, but it keeps the rocks clean for easy identification.

Special attractions: Owyhee Uplands Back Country Byway; DeLamar silver mine
Finding the site: From the intersection of US 95 and ID 55 at Marsing, drive 33 miles on US 95 to near Sheaville. If coming from Oregon, drive 11.5 miles north on US 95. Just north of Sheaville, head east on Silver City Road and drive 0.7 mile. Turn right onto Old US 95 for 0.6 mile, and resume on Silver City Road for 0.6 mile. This road is now named Cow Creek Road at the Idaho border; go another 4.9 miles to the giant wash in the road. To reach Site B, drive another 1.9 miles toward Silver City and note the giant boulders on the left. If you are continuing to Silver City or South Mountain, drive about 6.2 miles farther southeast to pick up Silver City Road.

Rockhounding

Everyone will find material here, despite the fact that the area has been searched for decades. There may be source material in seams in the upper cliffs above Cow Creek, but I've stuck to the washes, poking around in most of the gulches that reach the main road and trying anything not gated that leads into the hills. The agate here is quite colorful, running from a milky white to reddish, yellow, blue, and clear. There is vivid red jasper, bright yellow jasper, and mixtures in between. The petrified wood can be disappointing—some may be porous, dull, and gray—but a few pieces clearly show the growth rings and knotholes that mark good wood, and sizes can be quite impressive.

Look for the big boulders at Site B.

Most times when I get back to camp or home and inspect my sample bag, I find one or two jasper or agate pieces that show signs of knapping. This, incidentally, is why rockhounds are allowed to pick up artifacts "incidental" to our primary activity.

The wash at Site A is seasonal, but it can be a big help in bringing the colors to life. At Site B, rockhounds have been taking swings at the big boulders and chipping off the light blue chalcedony. It's a bit porous, but there are nice pieces yet to come.

There are more locales near Wagontown. If you continue to Silver City, you'll drive to the end of Cow Creek Road and come to a junction. From here you can see the massive DeLamar silver mine to the south. If you feel adventurous, don't take Silver City Road yet; instead take the unnamed spur off to the left from the junction for about 1.1 miles and veer right another 1.3 miles to pass two areas with some good "bog wood"—a black or clear chalcedony (Ream 2012, 14). Otherwise, continue to Silver City. About 0.5 mile farther there is a good locale for more bog wood, with good color. Along Jordan Creek you can pan for gold if you find an unclaimed spot; there is plenty of color in this creek, as well as more rockhounding for petrified wood, jasper, and quartz. There are also reports of cassiterite, tin oxide (SnO_2), in the gravels of Jordan Creek.

This is snake country, so beware. Also, a thunderstorm can turn these roads into treacherous gumbo. Use caution.

Nice blue chalcedony from the big boulders at Site B

64. Silver City

See map on page 165.

Land type: Alpine forest, brushy creeks, sagebrush hillsides
County: Owyhee
GPS: A: 43.02592, -116.73284; 6,131 feet (Slaughterhouse Gulch)
     B: 43.01921, -116.73185; 6,246 feet (Morningstar Mine)
     C: 43.00793, -116.74661; 6,487 feet (Long Gulch)
Best season: July and August
Land manager: BLM–Owyhee
Material: Cassiterite, gold, garnet, quartz, calcite
Tools: Screens and gold pan in creek; geology pick elsewhere
Vehicle: 4WD suggested; even main roads are rough and steep.

The DeLamar silver mine's distinctive white and red cliffs are visible from many miles away.

Accommodations: Developed campground in Silver City; primitive camping on national forest lands throughout the area

Special attractions: Owyhee Uplands Back Country Byway; Idaho Hotel in "downtown" Silver City (bring your camera)

Finding the site: The roads into Silver City aren't advisable for RVs or trailers. To come in from the west, turn off US 95 at Jordan Valley and head east on Yturri Boulevard, then follow Long Ridge Road about 25 miles to the turn for Silver City. From Murphy, which is on ID 78 south of Nampa, head east on ID 78 about 5 miles to the Ridge Road/Silver City Road turnoff. There are two historical markers here, so it's easy to spot the turn. Follow Silver City Road for about 20 miles and turn left to Silver City at the Ruby City/Slaughterhouse Gulch rest area. This is Site A. To reach Site B at the Morningstar dumps, drive 0.6 mile toward Silver City; turn sharply left onto Morning Star Mine Road and go up the hill. Don't circle back to the main road. To reach Site C, start at the Idaho Hotel and drive north on Jordan Street for 1 block, then turn left onto Washington Street. Go about 1 block and veer right; drive 0.2 mile, then turn left and inch your way up to Site C at the old camp, about 1 mile. There are more dumps in another 0.1 mile.

Rockhounding

Site A is the open area at historic Ruby City, with a restroom and generous parking area. ATVs use this spot quite a bit, as there are a lot of trails to follow through the granite outcrops. Rockhounds search this area for quartz crystals, also calcite. My reading is from above the road, where the ATVs won't bother you, but the whole area is worth exploring if it isn't busy. If you can, try to hook up with a field trip sponsored by the Idaho Gem Club or Owyhee Gem & Mineral Club to this area.

Jordan Creek offers opportunities for panning gold and nice red garnets plus a rarity: cassiterite, or tin oxide. I say *opportunities,* but it will take a lot of digging and screening and panning (or sluicing) to come up with the pea-size gray cassiterite. Not so for the garnet, which is plentiful. There are good exposures of bedrock along Jordan Creek in the gulch that winds to the west to the DeLamar Mine, so look for traps and crevices to exploit.

Site B, a good spot for quartz crystals, is at the old Morningstar Mine, just to the west as you drive into Silver City. It's been hit hard over the years, and most of the quartz is milky white, but look for good terminations at least.

Quartz veins in this district tended to run for thousands of feet, prompting interesting battles beneath the surface as miners intersected competing

Samples from the dumps around Silver City—green malachite for sure, and possible silver ore in the quartz on the left

workings. Ore minerals include argentite, electrum, ruby silver, tetrahedrite, galena, pyrite, marcasite, and chalcopyrite. Secondary minerals include owyheeite, an ore with lead, silver, antimony, and bismuth found at the Poorman Mine.

To reach Site C out Long Gulch, turn off Washington Street at the old pharmacy, drive past some old mill ruins, and check the tailings about 0.7 mile out of town. The camp still has some structures up at Site C, and you can access quite a bit of tailings here; roam around and bust up anything that looks like quartz with rusty staining to potentially get to ore minerals.

65. War Eagle Mountain

See map on page 165.

Land type: Alpine forest, brushy creeks, sagebrush hillsides
County: Owyhee
GPS: A: 43.01095, -116.69891; 7,305 feet (pits along road)
    B: 43.00573, -116.69833; 7,607 feet (pits)
    C: 43.00327, -116.70483; 7,791 feet (tailings)
    D: 43.00453, -116.70701; 7,724 feet (tailings)
Best season: July and August
Land manager: BLM–Owyhee
Material: Quartz crystals mostly; metal ores possible
Tools: Screens and gold pan in creek; geology pick elsewhere
Vehicle: 4WD required
Accommodations: Developed campground in Silver City; primitive camping on national forest lands throughout the War Eagle Mountain area

Silver City is a long ways down from this view.

Special attractions: Owyhee Uplands Back Country Byway; Idaho Hotel in "downtown" Silver City (bring your camera)

Finding the site: From the Idaho hotel in Silver City, drive north on Jordan Street 0.7 mile and turn right onto Silver City Road. Drive 0.5 mile and turn right (south) onto the road to War Eagle Mountain. If coming from Murphy, you'd pick Silver City Road from ID 78. There are two historical markers here, so it's easy to spot the turn. Follow Silver City Road for about 18.6 miles to the turn. Drive up the mountain about 2.2 miles to reach Site A. To reach Site B, drive another 0.9 mile. To reach Site C, drive up the mountain another 0.4 mile, swing right, and continue looping around to your right about 0.2 mile to the tailings. Site D is just up the hill a few hundred feet to the northwest.

Rockhounding

War Eagle Mountain has decent enough quartz crystals on this southwestern side, and it's worth the drive up to check them. You can see the top of the mountain above you here due to the radio towers. At each of these stops, you should be able to find small clusters of quartz crystals stuck together; singles are rare. You will probably have good luck just inspecting the rubble, but a hammer will come in handy too. Look for any signs of mineralization, such as rusty staining or metallic streaks.

There are several active mines in the area that you should stay clear of. We met a crew of exploration geologists looking for gold showings on the northeast side, and they confirmed that the quartz was where we expected it to be. Feel free to inspect any outcrops you see at the top of the hill, and be sure to venture a little to the west for the view of Silver City, far below. Site A was the Oro Fino Mine. Site B may have been part of the San Juan Mine, while Sites C and D were probably part of the Stormy Hill complex.

Stubby little quartz crystals from near the top of War Eagle Mountain at Site D

66. Reynolds Creek

See map on page 165.

Land type: Diggings in open sagebrush, low rolling hills
County: Owyhee
GPS: 43.21440, -116.74170; 3,956 feet
Best season: Spring and fall; avoid hot weather.
Land manager: BLM–Bruneau
Material: Petrified wood
Tools: Pick and shovel, geology pick
Vehicle: 4WD suggested but not necessary
Accommodations: Open BLM lands south of here on Democrat Road for primitive camping; developed camping at Givens Hot Springs
Special attractions: Owyhee Uplands Back Country Byway; Snake River Birds of Prey National Conservation Area
Finding the site: From ID 78 0.1 mile west of Murphy, take Rabbit Creek Road south about 1 mile, where the road becomes Reynolds Creek Stage Road. Continue for 5.1 miles, then turn right to stay on Reynolds Creek Stage Road. Drive another 4.5 miles and turn right onto a primitive road. You will have to open and close the gate. Drive on this road about 1.1 miles until you see the next gate. There

Digging area at Reynolds Creek. Gem clubs have hit this spot hard over the years.

is a wide spot for parking to the right, and the grass is beaten down here. Park and walk to the left, up the hill and across the flat at the top to the diggings. When you make the turn onto the unmarked dirt road, you are about 0.9 mile from Reynolds; if you miss the turn, simply backtrack. You can also reach the small town of Reynolds from ID 78 by taking Upper Reynolds Creek Road, about 18 miles east of Marsing.

Rockhounding

You should see extensive diggings, as local rock clubs have used this site at least once a year in the past. When we visited again in 2019, however, it looked desolated. Take a leisurely walk around the area and look for small chips of wood, and hope they lead to bigger pieces. Determine a good spot to start digging, then use a pick or shovel to scrape dirt from the wood layer. The overburden is less than a foot deep, and it can be as little as 4 to 6 inches.

Much of the wood here is spotty and soft and thus doesn't take a decent polish, but if you can get into the right zone, you should find good, hard wood. Otherwise, you're left with some very nice display pieces. The grain and habit of the wood show off well, and there is a lot to go around. Even though local clubs include this site in their annual field trip schedules, Reynolds Creek should be productive for years to come.

As usual out here in the desert, I also spotted lots of rounded river rock composed of agate, milk-white quartz, and jasper. A nice orange chalcedony full of bubbles encrusted some of the boulders, so I brought it home too. If you like zeolites, check out the dark basalts along ID 78 where it crosses Sinker Creek. The zone is about 6 miles west of the turn to Oreana. Be sure to be extremely careful about parking and about falling rock; it is best to follow the outcrop south and away from the highway.

Fisher (see bibliography) shows additional fossil locales in this general area. Note: Every time I've been out here in spring or early summer, I've seen giant black crickets on many of the roads. They're kinda creepy, all moving in the same direction, but basically harmless.

Striking bubbly chalcedony from the petrified wood pits

67. Tinsdale Road

See map on page 190.

Land type: Open sagebrush, low rolling hills
County: Owyhee
GPS: A: 42.76342, -115.89222; 3,012 feet (diggings)
    B: 42.75586, -115.90020; 3,027 feet (ash beds)
Best season: Year-round, except dead of winter and highest heat of summer
Land manager: BLM–Bruneau
Material: Petrified wood, agate, jasper
Tools: Geology pick
Vehicle: Any, but 4WD allows you to explore side roads better.

Petrified wood is on the ground and in the ash beds at Site B.

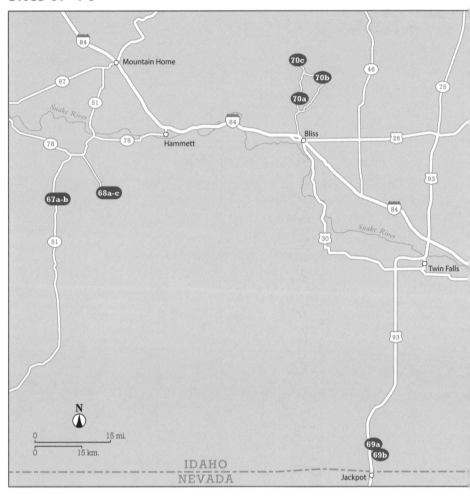

Accommodations: Developed camping at Bruneau Dunes State Park; RV parks in Mountain Home; open primitive camping at Site B and nearby areas on BLM lands
Special attractions: Owyhee Uplands Back Country Byway. Bruneau has full services and interesting old buildings.
Finding the site: From Mountain Home, head south on ID 51. Cross the Snake River and drive through Bruneau. Do not take the ID 78 turn; stay on ID 51, headed south. About 8.9 miles from the junction with ID 78, look for a decent gravel road headed east named Last Frontier Road. About 1.1 miles in, you will find a turn to the right and head over to the white ash beds. To reach Site B, return to ID 51 and turn left. Go about 1.1 miles south and look for a left turn (west); drive about 0.25 mile and stay left. This is a known spot for petrified wood; it's very productive, although the quality of the wood isn't great.

Rockhounding

This is a great area to just park and search. Site A is also called the Bruneau Woodpile (Ream 2012, 42). There are lots of spots where you'll see digging in the soil, and in places the productive layer can be covered by 3 feet of soil. The soil can be compacted and tough to dig into, so you may be better off widening someone else's pit. The wood is more limb-like here, and is better petrified than at Site B. Give yourself time to roam around and look for fragments that you might be able to trace up the hill, and work wherever you see ruts that may be signs of multiple vehicles reaching a good site.

The wood at Site B was once bigger but has fragmented into shards. Some of them are quite attractive, so make sure you hit both spots.

The sites listed here work for starters, but any road you choose to take off ID 51 offers opportunities. I had good luck at some white cliffs along the Civilian Conservation Corps (CCC) road and all along Grasmere Road. Any time you find a gulch or seasonal streambed, you have a chance to find wood, opal, jasper, quartz, etc. In some spots the rocks are rounded and appear to have been worked by water. In other areas the material is more angular and hasn't moved very far. The wood seems to be associated with the white ash beds, if you care to dig. There are probably some agate and jasper seams in between the lava flows dotting the nearby hillsides.

Some specimens look like branches.

The literature suggests a locale farther down ID 51 at Riddle, near Blue Creek Bridge. This area is now private, however, and closed to rockhounding.

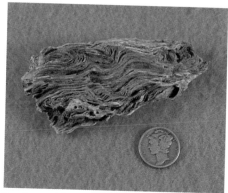

Fragile wood from Site B

68. Bruneau River

See map on page 190.
Land type: Creek beds, gulches
County: Owyhee
GPS: A: 42.78550, -115.70429; 2,718 feet (road bed)
     B: 42.77763, -115.69322; 2,781 feet (gully along road)
     C: 42.76519, -115.67897; 3,198 feet (gravel pit)
Best season: Late spring and fall; avoid summer heat.
Land manager: BLM–Bruneau
Material: Jasper, quartz, agate, petrified wood
Tools: Geology pick
Vehicle: Any, but must be able to handle gravel roads with washboards and sharp rocks
Accommodations: Plenty of primitive camping on open BLM lands nearby; developed camping at Bruneau Dunes State Park; RV parks in Mountain Home
Special attractions: Owyhee Uplands Back Country Byway; Bruneau Canyon Scenic Overlook
Finding the site: From Mountain Home, head south on ID 51 toward Bruneau. Cross the Snake River; just as you enter Bruneau, turn left onto Hot Springs Road, following the signs for the Bruneau Canyon overlook, which is a must-see. After 8.2 miles the main road turns left and becomes Clover 3 Creek Road. Site A is about 8.6 miles from Bruneau, off to the left on a dirt road. Site B is about 9.4 miles from Bruneau, on the right. Site C is a large gravel pit about 10.7 miles from Bruneau and on the left.

Rockhounding

Look for impressive collections of washed, rounded river rock as you leave Bruneau. The various road cuts sometimes show bedded pebble conglomerates waiting to fall apart. These deposits probably have less to do with the Bruneau River than with an ancestral Snake River or ancient Lake Lahontan. Whatever the source, the material is excellent. As soon as you clear the ranches down in the bottomland and the road really goes up, you'll see the different sites for collecting. There is good parking at these spots.

There was a time when rockhounds far and wide flocked to the Bruneau River to dig an amazing variety of material. Some of the world's most

The large pit at Site C yields plenty of rounded river rock.

picturesque jasper, with bubbles and spheres in endless variety, came from the area at the confluence of the Jarbidge and Bruneau Rivers. Alas, there are at least six active claims in the area, with no plans for public fee digging. Fisher (see bibliography) reports that he collected from the river, outside the claim boundaries, and had good luck. I've had rockhounds tell me that they found good picture jasper in nearby gulches as well, but they wouldn't tell me where. I had two flat tires before I even reached the turnoff to the Bruneau River, so that locale didn't make the cut, but don't let that discourage you.

Beckwith's old Indian Bathtub locale (see bibliography), which is right on the Bruneau River, once yielded amethyst-lined geodes. That site is not only exhausted but also on private land. We've had good luck finding jasper and petrified wood on nearby CCC/Grasmere Road, and just about every side road yields petrified wood, agate, and jasper. At Site A, park and roam around on the public land; there is a gulch coming in from the southeast you should check as well. Site B is a nice gully that gets hit hard but still produces. Site C is a giant pit with a large selection of rounded river rock on the north wall and plenty more on the ground. Look for large pieces that you might be able to saw into slices.

Agate and petrified limb from Site B

69. Rabbit Springs

See map on page 190.
Land type: Open sagebrush, rolling hills
County: Twin Falls
GPS: A: 42.05603, -114.65084; 5,803 feet (crossing)
B: 42.06492, -114.67426; 5,488 feet (pits)
Best season: Early spring through late fall; avoid dead of winter.
Land manager: BLM–Burley
Material: Fluorescent geodes, agate
Tools: Heavy hammer, geology pick
Vehicle: Any
Accommodations: Primitive camping allowed on open BLM lands; developed camping along nearby Salmon Falls Creek Reservoir; casinos in Jackpot, Nevada
Special attractions: Thousand Springs Scenic Byway; casinos at Jackpot, Nevada; Salmon Falls Creek Reservoir
Finding the site: From I-84, take Twin Falls exit 173 and follow the signs to US 93 South. US 30/Addison Avenue will take you west to the turn for US 93; from the exit off US 30, Rabbit Springs is about 37 miles south on US 93. From Jackpot, Nevada, head north and cross the state line on US 93, then drive about 4.2 miles from the border. Park off to the west; there is room to pull off safely. If it doesn't look safe enough to you, exit on the road that leads east to a network of side tracks and park there. US 93 can be a busy road, so be prudent and stay well off the highway. The state police might ask you to leave if you aren't safely off the road.

Rockhounding

Broken, hollow geodes litter the ground here, and the diggings are both extensive and easy to spot. The eggs are weathering out of the basalt flows, but you don't need to get over to the highway road cut and impede traffic to find good material. Use your hammer to break up any suspect geodes, or (better idea) take them home to run through the saw.

The geode deposit stretches to the west, and there is reportedly more collecting down at the far southern end of nearby Salmon Falls Creek Reservoir, but this site will satisfy your appetite. Over on the east side of the highway, you can see a large bluff of basalt. Hike over and check for seams of a blue-gray

Pit of thundereggs from Rabbit Springs

Broken thundereggs are everywhere in these pits.

agate—the agate material is plentiful. Also, most of the gravel roads in this area have ample chunks of agate just waiting to be recovered. Nevada guidebooks list a spot south of Jackpot as well.

This locale is famous for material that fluoresces. If you bring a portable UV (black) light, you can detect the greenish glow of the chalcedony inside the thundereggs. A faint pink color also shows up.

70. Clover Creek

See map on page 190.

Land type: Lava plains, sagebrush hills

County: Gooding

GPS: A: 43.03272, -114.94787; 3,303 feet (bridge)

    B: 43.13810, -114.95741; 4,978 feet (top)

    C: 43.09249, -114.86144; 4,139 feet (chalk mine)

Best season: Late spring through fall; avoid high runoff.

Land manager: BLM–Shoshone; some private land to avoid

Material: Agate, jasper, petrified and opalized wood

Tools: Geology pick if hiking; heavy hammer

Vehicle: 4WD suggested to cut down on hiking

Accommodations: Primitive camping on BLM lands along Clover Creek Road, north of White Arrow Hot Springs; motel in Bliss; RV parks in Jerome and Hagerman

Special attractions: Sawtooth Scenic Byway; Thousand Springs Scenic Byway; numerous lava tubes, including Shoshone Ice Cave

Finding the site: From I-84, exit at Bliss and find First Avenue. Swing north onto First; as it leaves town it becomes Clover Creek Road. To reach Sites A and B, follow the road north for about 7 miles. Site A is at the bridge across the creek; look for a road that leads east just before you cross the bridge over Clover Creek. There are no fences, and you can see good gravel piles dropped by the braided stream. This is probably the easiest spot to search on Clover Creek, though there are a couple of spots downstream that are open, including one near some interesting lava bridges.

To reach Site B, continue on Clover Creek Road. For a brief detour, at about 0.4 mile beyond the bridge, look for a short dirt track leading east. Park here and search to the north for Crow Cave, an interesting lava tube. Back on the road, there is an intersection about 0.5 mile from the lava tube. The pavement appears to swing east, but that leads to a private ranch. You want to proceed onto gravel for about another 8.5 miles until you are at the top. Look for a cattle guard followed by a fairly decent road that goes down sharply to Clover Creek. If you trust your rig, you can drive on down, but most searchers walk from here. There are some gates to contend with; the road crosses the creek and leads past several prospects in the white ash beds.

Take the time to explore some of the lava tubes in the Clover Creek area.

To reach Site C, consider the options: You can backtrack toward Bliss and take 1300 Southeast, but it is a nasty little road that gets worse as it nears Bray Reservoir. Or you can come in from Gooding, following ID 46 north out of town and then taking 5 Mile Road (East 1300 South) to North Road. This 6.3-mile drive is still rough, but not as much of a threat to your tires. There is another lava tube at 43.01223, -114.83610 on Dead Horse Cave Road. This cave has concrete stairs going down, but there is a lot of broken glass on the ground.

At Site C, look for white ash beds along both sides of the road at the parking area. Clover Creek is far down below, but the hike isn't too bad. If your rig is up to it, the road goes on around the hill and gets much closer to the creek before the end of the trail. However, it's just as easy (and less nerve-racking) to park and hike to the dandy little gravel bars below the chalk mine.

Rockhounding

At each site, the prize material will be larger pieces of jasper and opalized or petrified wood. Smaller chunks of agate are also common, but they are probably remnants of the giant Pleistocene lakes that once filled these basins. The wood and jasper source is upper Clover Creek, reached via Site A. However, it's a long hike or bone-jarring drive, and my guess is that most collectors can make a nice trip out of the lava tubes and some easier creek walks.

Remember to avoid private land, and don't cross any posted fences to reach Clover Creek. You should be able to collect plenty of material from the creek if the water is low. A particularly wet spring can make some of the roads much more adventurous than you probably want, with creek and canal crossings especially exciting. The elevation is low enough in this area that you can collect in early spring, but the trade-off will be mud and creek crossings. Summer heat can be unbearable.

Small but highly polished wood fragment from Clover Creek

71. Big Wood River

See map on page 200.
Land type: River bottom
County: Blaine
GPS: 43.32954, -114.31918; 4,848 feet
Best season: Year-round, except dead of winter
Land manager: BLM–Shoshone
Material: Tumbler material, including quartz, agate, opal, chalcedony, jasper, petrified wood, granite
Tools: Geology pick

Even with a little snow on the ground, this can be a relaxing and rewarding stroll.

Sites 71–76

Vehicle: Any; site is right off US 20.

Accommodations: None at site; Stanton Crossing campground, just 0.3 mile east; primitive camping on open BLM lands to the north; developed camping at Magic Reservoir

Special attractions: Sawtooth Scenic Byway; Magic Reservoir

Finding the site: From Carey, drive about 20.5 miles west on US 20. From Shoshone, drive about 28.5 miles north on ID 75, then go 2.3 miles west on US 20. From Fairfield, drive east on US 20 about 23.7 miles. From Ketchum, drive about 26.2 miles south on ID 75 then 2.3 miles west on US 20.

Rockhounding

By the middle of April, these gravel bars can be ready to hunt, making them a nice early opportunity. Of all the spots I've searched in Idaho, the material here was some of the cleanest and easiest to find. There is a good campground called Stanton Crossing just 0.3 mile east, which gives you even more gravel access. The variety is outstanding, ranging from nice tumbled granites to milky quartz and colorful jasper. You can also find a variety of vein quartz, some with rusty staining, which hopefully originated in the gold country above Hailey and Ketchum. Red and yellow jaspers are the easiest to spot in the gray common rock here. For just plain rocks, notice the banded gneiss and chunky granite.

There is no fence here, so park off the road when you notice the gravel bars mere steps from the pavement. A game warden once came up to us here to check for fishing rods. It was right before the fishing season opened, and he seemed quite relieved that we were "just rockhounding."

There are more access points as you head north to Bellevue and Hailey, but considerable private land will frustrate you. My advice is to stick to this spot and get a good hike in. If you check during summer, wear short pants and sturdy sandals and you can repeatedly cross the creek.

Bring a gold pan and see if you can detect black sands and a little color. At the very least, you should be able to pan out some small red garnets.

Interesting jaspers from Big Wood River

72. Croy Creek

See map on page 200.
Land type: Riverbank, tailings piles
County: Blaine
GPS: A: 43.51668, -114.32221; 5,390 feet (river access)
    B: 43.45647, -114.43819; 5,854 feet (Liberty Gem Mine)
    C: 43.41548, -114.46348; 6,335 feet (Tip Top Mine)
Best season: Summer
Land manager: BLM–Shoshone
Material: Quartz vein material with sulfide ores such as galena and pyrite; rough quartz crystals
Tools: Heavy hammer, chisels
Vehicle: 4WD required for upper sites; roads are little more than ruts in places.
Accommodations: Primitive camping at site; developed spots (and more firewood) at Deer Creek Road to the north

The headframe is still standing at the Liberty Gem Mine.

Special attractions: Hailey Hot Springs resort on Croy Creek Road; Sawtooth Scenic Byway; Hailey, Ketchum, and Sun Valley

Finding the site: From ID 75 at Hailey, take Bullion Street west 0.4 mile and cross the bridge. Site A is the river access spot just outside of town; there are lots of gravels here, but try to find the spot where Croy Creek dumps into the Big Wood River. Beyond Site A, Bullion Street becomes Croy Creek Road. Site B is 7.6 miles from ID 75; look for a faint dirt track headed right (northwest). The tailings piles and a small collapsed wooden structure are visible from the road.

To reach Site C, drive 10.4 miles on Croy Creek Road from ID 75 to Richardson Summit, then take a left onto a poor road that leads along the ridge. Follow it around about 2.1 miles to the ridge that separates two major workings. The tailings, which I believe are part of the Tip Top Mine, are easily visible. Just before reaching the tailings, I had to dodge a part of the road that was washed out. That meant driving down (and back up) a very steep stretch. You may be better off parking and walking; the tailings make an easy landmark.

Rockhounding

The Hailey area saw considerable mining in the past, and numerous prospects and pits dot the land out on Croy Creek Road. This area is underlain by the Idaho Batholith, which is in turn cut by aplite, pegmatite, and lamprophyre dikes. Most of the Tertiary basalt here has been eroded away. Gold occurs in the quartz veins, with up to four times as much silver as gold, by weight. The usual ratio is 16 to 1, so the ore is rich in silver.

The Red Cloud Mine is up Bullion Gulch, which is described in the literature as the Mineral Hill Mining District. Red Elephant Mine Road is clearly marked with a road sign, so check it out. The Democrat Mine is up Democrat Gulch, but in early summer the creek is rushing right down the road; you'll have to go in on foot. Colorado Gulch Road leads southeast from Croy Creek Road and leads to several prospects in the hills, although an ATV would be better than a Jeep.

At Site A you'll mostly find tumbler material, but it's a nice break on a hot day. If you want luxury, try Hailey Hot Springs.

At Site B look for quartz veins as well as red-stained quartz outcrops, and bring a big hammer to bust up boulders. Most of the pyrite and sulfide material oxidizes quickly, so you need to reach deep, dry areas of solid rock to get good sulfides.

This interesting boulder disintegrated with one hammer blow; the specimens were extremely dense.

Site C marks the Camas Mining District and the Tip Top Mine. This locale offers an impressive quartz outcrop, and I found numerous crude quartz crystals in the area. There appear to be small black hornblende crystals as well.

Note: Site C is only 3.5 miles as the crow flies north of Moonstone Mountain. It might be worth checking out.

73. Little Wood River

See map on page 200.
Land type: Creek beds and sagebrush hills above reservoir
County: Blaine
GPS: A: 43.42140, -114.01258; 5,118 feet (access point)
      B: 43.42370, -114.02801; 5,249 feet (reservoir)
Best season: Any, but late summer is best after the runoff recedes.
Land manager: BLM–Shoshone
Material: Quartz, agate, chalcedony, jasper, petrified wood; sulfides in some of the massive quartz
Tools: Heavy hammer, chisels

This dry creek bed may look nondescript, but there is good agate, jasper, and petrified wood here, some of it quite large.

Vehicle: Any; road is paved and well-maintained gravel, though there are some potholes and washboards to contend with.

Accommodations: None at site; primitive camping on open BLM lands to the north; fee camping at Little Wood Reservoir

Special attractions: Sawtooth Scenic Byway. Carey has full services.

Finding the site: At the north end of Carey on US 20, look to the left for signs leading to Little Wood Reservoir. Drive north about 9.1 miles on Little Wood Reservoir Road and start looking for a slight right turn. Park in a small grass parking area along the creek where the road dips to allow the creek to pass underneath. Look for the green and white "Access yes!" sign. Walk through the gate to the creek (be sure to close the gate behind you). This is Site A.

To reach Site B, drive up through the camping area to the dam; make your way to the southwest end and then park.

Rockhounding

Bring a big hammer and break up rocks, or just surface collect whatever piques your interest. At Site A we first ranged somewhat north, away from the river, exploring the small creek that comes in roughly from the northwest. We found agate and jasper in abundance, and some of the pieces were very large. We also found some bulky quartz that broke into nice display pieces and picked up petrified wood that hadn't been moved a great distance. After a while, we turned to the banks of the Little Wood River itself and found similar material, though considerably more rounded and polished.

A good chunk of agate from Site A

At Site B, search the hillside for tube agate. Drive or hike throughout the hillside area and look for diggings or disturbed earth.

Little Wood Reservoir was noted by Beckwith (see bibliography), and rockhounds have scoured the hills around here with good success. There is more agate and petrified wood along the west edge of the reservoir, and it's all open for collecting, with the usual cautions about private property.

74. Cold Springs Creek

See map on page 200.

Land type: Sagebrush hills, stream gravels
County: Blaine
GPS: A: 43.48815, -114.05551; 5,317 feet (camping)
    B: 43.49731, -114.05716; 5,336 feet (gravels)
    C: 43.50225, -114.05162; 5,433 feet (agate, jasper in wash)
    D: 43.50761, -114.08758; 5,551 feet (creek, hills)
Best season: Summer; high elevation sees considerable snow.
Land manager: BLM–Shoshone
Material: Agate, quartz, jasper, chalcedony; occasional petrified wood
Tools: Heavy hammer
Vehicle: 4WD suggested; road is rough in places.
Accommodations: Primitive camping at site; developed campgrounds at Little Wood Reservoir and above Muldoon
Special attractions: Sawtooth Scenic Byway; Muldoon Summit
Finding the site: From Airport Lane in Carey, drive north on Main Street 0.7 mile and turn left onto Little Wood Reservoir Road. Drive 12.3 miles, past Site 73, and then continue on what is now Flat Top Road. Drive 1.8 miles, turn left, and drive 1.3 miles back to the creek. There is camping here, with gravels along the creek. To reach Site B, resume driving north about 0.6 mile, but before you cross the bridge, look for faint tracks leading to the creek on the right; drive to the parking area there. To reach Site C, resume north for 0.5 mile then turn right onto Muldoon Canyon Road. Drive about 0.6 mile to the wash that drops below the road. To reach Site D, return west, back across the creek on Muldoon Canyon Road. Go back to the north after crossing the creek, then stay on the main road, headed west, for a total of 2.2 miles. Site D is where the road crosses the creek.

Rockhounding

I've had good luck throughout this area, so if the sites listed here are wiped out, feel free to find more spots by hiking around—the farther from the road, the better the chances. Most of the hillside washes are worth exploring, and if you get lucky, you might find agate seams or jasperized outcrops to attack with a heavy hammer. If you run into posted areas, respect them, and don't cross any signed fences. There is plenty of room to roam, and no need to trespass. The creeks at Sites A, B, and D are about equal in approach—search far and wide, attack with a hammer to get that ringing sound of hard quartz, and take your time while still covering a lot of ground. Site C is a dry wash, but it holds good material that is quite large.

Even without hard-rock mining in bedrock, this area is very productive for quartz, agate, jasper, and petrified wood. Most every stream, gulch, or washout contains material, and if you find an area with bigger rocks, you should be able to locate excellent cutting material. The stream gravels are always productive as well. Every time you cross the creek, check it for gravel accumulations, and check any side roads that lead to water. For example, after backtracking from Site C to reach Site D, there is a road headed north that

Muldoon Creek in the Cold Springs area contains loads of interesting cobbles and boulders.

Giant-size jasper specimen from Site C

parallels the western side of the small creek coming in, and it's worth checking. Also, be advised that the hunting grounds extend for several miles west from Site D.

The jasper runs red and yellow, with occasional brown pieces mixed in. The quality is good—the jasper is hard and shows the characteristic fracture marks of gem-quality material. The agate ranges from milky white to clear, with banding common. Bring along a geology pick to pry rocks out of the dirt—you may only recognize a tip projecting out, and then discover it is a very large piece.

75. Muldoon Creek

See map on page 200.

Land type: Creek beds, sagebrush hills
County: Blaine
GPS: A: 43.56873, -113.91454; 6,462 feet (creek crossing)
     B: 43.57826, -113.91558; 6,226 feet (gulch)
Best season: Summer through early fall
Land manager: BLM–Shoshone; USDA Forest Service–Sawtooth National Forest
Material: Agate, jasper, chalcedony, petrified wood, barite
Tools: Geology pick
Vehicle: 4WD suggested; roads are rough but passable.
Accommodations: Primitive camping on BLM lands; Copper Creek Campground is along the creek once you reach the USFS boundary.
Special attractions: Sawtooth Scenic Byway; Craters of the Moon National Monument
Finding the site: From Airport Lane in Carey, drive north on Main Street 0.7 mile and turn left onto Little Wood Reservoir Road. Drive 12.3 miles, past Site 73, and then continue on what is now Flat Top Road (this route will skip Site 74). Alternatively, you can take in Site 74 and use Muldoon Canyon Road to head east. If you stay on Flat Top Road, you'll travel 2.3 miles then pick up Muldoon Canyon Road; stay right and drive 6.1 miles east. This is Site A. There is no sign for Muldoon, which is where Copper Creek joins Muldoon Creek. Site B is 0.8 mile farther, and the turnoff for the barite mine is in another 1.8 miles. The USFS boundary is about 2.3 miles north of Site A.

Rockhounding

This area has been a fixture in rockhounding guides for decades, but the hills and gulches are still very productive. The big problem has been the steady advent of private land, which rendered obsolete many of the lower hillsides mentioned by Beckwith. Ream (see bibliography) has good, more recent details for this area. The readings I recorded here were rewarding, but don't limit your search if you don't find material as soon as you step out of the car. I barely scratched the surface. You can look in any gully, gulch, intermittent creek, or gravel accumulation for material with reasonable hope. Once you

Extensive gravels along Muldoon Creek

find something interesting, look up and see if there are diggings or ledges above you.

My favorite material here is a banded agate, with some blue tinting. I also found plenty of clear tubular agate, though it was usually small. The jasper here can be spectacular, ranging from yellow to red, and hard. Petrified wood is not common, but I stumbled across it once in a while, usually in the gravels of Muldoon Creek. Every chance you get to cross the creek, be sure to check the gravels, and check any dry washes that look choked with cobbles too.

Fisher lists a barite mine (43.60141, -113.90352) on his DVD, so it's a good opportunity for barite crystals; he reports ammonite fossils from the mine area as well.

Agate chunks from Muldoon Creek will take an excellent polish.

76. Fish Creek Reservoir

See map on page 200.

Land type: Sagebrush and rolling foothills, reservoir banks, creek beds
County: Blaine
GPS: 43.41659, -113.83515; 5,217 feet (campground)
Best season: Summer through fall
Land manager: BLM–Shoshone
Material: Jasper, agate, petrified wood; obsidian chips
Tools: Geology pick
Vehicle: Any; excellent gravel road to reservoir
Accommodations: Fee camping at Fish Creek Reservoir; ample opportunities for primitive camping on BLM lands north on Fish Creek Road, but avoid private ranches.
Special attractions: Sawtooth Scenic Byway; Craters of the Moon National Monument
Finding the site: From Carey, at the intersection with US 26, drive east on US 20 about 7.8 miles and look for a well-marked left (north) turn to Fish Creek Reservoir. Take this gravel road about 3.8 miles toward the reservoir, but turn left onto an unmarked road. Drive about 1.1 miles, staying left, and drive under the face of the dam and back up, curling south. At the fork, you can drive another 0.2 mile due

View of the dam from camp

south, to the edge of the rim overlooking the outflow, which is a good camping spot, or you can continue around to the west of the reservoir and parallel this small creek for about 1.2 miles, into the hills. Be sure to leave all gates as you found them.

Rockhounding

The access road to the bottom of the dam crosses material that is really big and uninteresting, probably fill. The banks around the reservoir can be too muddy to walk on if the spring is particularly wet—the hillsides are a better bet. At the coordinates we found plenty of small material such as agate and jasper, as well as some petrified wood. There were also multiple obsidian chips, as though there was an arrowhead factory here at one time.

Farther past the official reservoir campground, try a left turn on West Fork Fish Creek Road and find a couple places to search where the road crosses the creek or gets close to it. Just about any gravel accumulation out here is likely to have something worth taking home. The trick is to find tumbler-ready material that is already smoothed a little or, if that doesn't work, to find freshly broken material. Bring your hammer not only to pry rocks from the dirt but also to break up the larger material.

Look for nice red jasper, sometimes intermixed with tan or yellow bands in a striking contrast. Agate and chalcedony are also common, though the agate is not particularly showy. Petrified wood is elusive.

West Fork Fish Creek Road has good material for quite a ways, so feel free to check it out as far as you care to go. There are some prospects by a cemetery on the topo map for the area. Also, the main stem of Fish Creek carries good material. If you find yourself discovering larger chunks, you might be closing in on the source material, so scan the hillsides above you.

Paleozoic rocks in the Long Canyon area below Fish Creek Reservoir are said to contain graptolite fossils and base metals; search the internet for USGS Bulletin 2064-KK. Farther east on the south and east slopes of Blizzard Mountain, there were several lode prospects. The Paymaster Mine at 43.48059, -113.65933 yielded zinc, lead, silver, gold, and copper, for example.

Assorted material from west of Fish Creek Reservoir

77. Big Southern Butte

See map on page 215.

Land type: Old cinder pit in sagebrush desert, immense rhyolite dome

County: Butte

GPS: A: 43.38123, -112.98796; 5,177 feet (cinder pit)

B: 43.39824, -113.04051; 7,023 feet (hang glider launch)

Best season: Summer; snows can linger on top of butte.

Land manager: BLM–Upper Snake

Material: Cinders in pit; obsidian on mountain

Tools: Geology pick

Vehicle: 4WD for driving to top of butte; sturdy rig required even for run to pit

Accommodations: Primitive camping at both sites; motels and RV parks at Arco

Special attractions: Sacajawea Historic Byway; Atomic City felt like it belonged in a *Mad Max* movie.

Finding the site: My way in was via Atomic City, a throwback to the Cold War days when understanding the power of the atom was a huge deal. Turn off US 26 at the sign for Atomic City; there is a decaying cafe at this turnoff. From Atomic City,

The cinder pit at Site A is open for collecting, unlike Craters of the Moon National Monument.

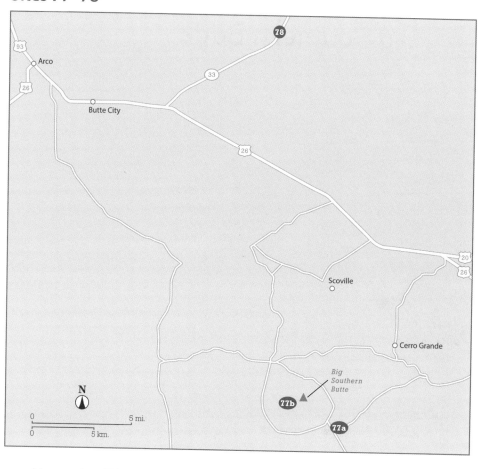

drive south on Taber Road about 1.7 miles to Big Butte Road. Stay on this road past the railroad tracks for a total of about 10.7 miles. Site A's deep red cinder pit is off to your right about 0.25 mile away.

To continue to Site B, drive past the pit to the junction with Big Butte/ Springfield Road, skip the turn onto the very rough Frenchglen Road, and keep circling Big Southern Butte. After about 7.1 miles, you'll come to a settlement/ junction and probably be greeted by several barking dogs. I came in from Atomic City, but you can also get here via Arco if you have a good map of the area. The road up to Site B is rough, so don't try it unless your rig is up to the task. The hang glider launch site is about 3.9 miles up the road, or you can drive all the way to the top, about 5.1 miles. It is extremely steep in places.

Be cautious about trying to drive in the flats all the way around the butte. Out on the northeast side, I got off on a pair of ruts that seemed like they dated to

Breathtaking view from atop the butte

the Oregon Trail days—only to learn later that they actually did. I was driving on Goodale's Cutoff, and it was such a calamity that I didn't have time to search out the obsidian locale.

Rockhounding

After hiking all over Craters of the Moon National Monument for the better part of a morning and enduring the endless "No Collecting" signs, I decided to include this cinder pit, since it is completely open. I found nice samples of cinder with swirls and streaks, plus one decent "bomb" spewed out about 40 yards from the center.

The drive up Big Southern Butte is impressive, with a great view from the top. There isn't much to collect, but it was an irresistible drive, so we did it; you should too, if your vehicle can handle it. Big Southern Butte is only about 300,000 years old, and rises nearly 2,500 feet above the surrounding plains.

I don't have an exact location for the best obsidian up here, but archaeologists have tracked artifacts made with this material for hundreds of miles in all directions. The literature points to Webb Spring, which drains to the north and requires an uphill hike from Frenchglen Road; refer to Google Earth for more information if you want to make the trek. This is supposed to be one of the better obsidian locales in Idaho, the other being Obsidian Gulch, a tributary of Bear Gulch just north of West Camas Creek, east of Spencer. I have been skunked both times here, but maybe you'll have better luck.

78. Arco Hills

See map on page 215.
Land type: Sagebrush hills
County: Butte
GPS: 43.66258, -113.05468; 5,177 feet
Best season: Year-round
Land manager: BLM–Upper Snake
Material: Permian fossils in limestone
Tools: Hammer, chisels
Vehicle: Any; 4WD suggested for exploring
Accommodations: Primitive camping at site
Special attractions: Arco has full services; Craters of the Moon National Monument is a must-see.
Finding the site: From Arco, head east on US 20/26 about 7.5 miles, then swing north onto ID 33. This highway is also numbered ID 22 and ID 88. Go about 7 miles and look for an unnamed turnoff to the left. Park safely anywhere; we found a spot about 0.1 mile from the highway that was a faint intersection and parked

There is easy access to the limestone hills right out of town.

Clams and sponges are common in the Arco limestones.

there. Walk farther up the hill and inspect the large outcrop. I found horn coral immediately.

Rockhounding

The Arco Hills are noted for Late Mississippian and Permian fossils, mostly brachiopods and horn corals. Geologists have identified at least fifteen different brachiopods from the Arco Hills Formation. There are so many limestone outcrops to search, you could stay busy here for a long time. I liked this spot because it was right off the highway. Equivalent rocks exist in Wyoming, Montana, and Utah.

I did find fossils in a couple other places that weren't as easy to get to. Roads out here tend to deteriorate quickly, so I don't recommend doing much four-wheeling out in the Arco Hills unless you have a good vehicle that can handle the bumps, dust, and sharp rocks. If you have the right vehicle, try using Arco Pass Road to reach coordinates 43.73954, -113.261956, via Sheep Camp Road. The Pass Road will take you even higher into the hills. Road 557 leads to Howe Peak then across to US 93; there is a lot of limestone to explore that way.

If you enjoy fossil hunting, try a web search for "Arco Hills Formation" to locate the appropriate papers, some being quite recent. Jack Wright Canyon, Mahogany Canyon, Arco Pass, and Sheep Camp Roads, among others, will take you up, over, around, and through these massive limestone deposits. East Grand Avenue downtown will take you to Highland Drive, and you can easily reach the hills overlooking town.

By early fall the colors are magnificent, the temperatures have dropped enough to be tolerable, and the roads are still easy to navigate. All of your usual backcountry cautions apply: Bring lots of water, plan for the worst, let someone know what you're up to, etc.

79. Trail Creek

See map on page 220.

Land type: Alpine forest, road cuts

County: A and B: Blaine; C and D: Custer

GPS: A: 43.73098, -114.30987; 6,125 feet (gravels)

    B: 43.80743, -114.25837; 7,558 feet (graptolites)

    C: 43.85132, -114.25351; 7,850 feet (drusy quartz)

    D: 43.84641, -114.20464; 8,036 feet (Phi Kappa Mine)

Best season: Late summer; don't drive up to Trail Creek Pass during periods of heavy rain or snow.

Large quartz vein near the Phi Kappa Mine

Sites 79–87

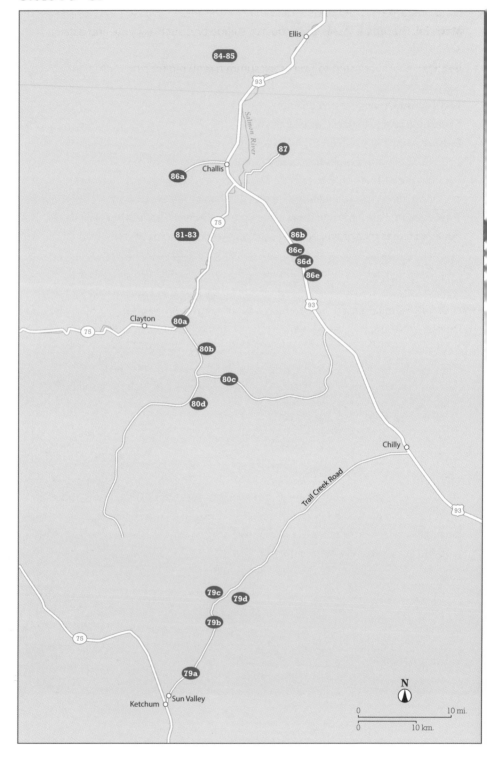

Land manager: USDA Forest Service–Sawtooth National Forest

Material: Graptolite fossils, drusy quartz; sulfide ores such as pyrite and galena

Tools: Heavy hammer, chisels

Vehicle: 4WD suggested to Trail Creek summit; required for side trips up Phi Kappa Creek and Little Fall Creek

Accommodations: Primitive camping at Site C and on national forest lands throughout the area; developed campsites at Phi Kappa Creek and Boundary Campground

Special attractions: Sawtooth Scenic Byway; Sun Valley and Ketchum

Finding the site: From Ketchum on ID 75, proceed east on Third Street, which becomes Sun Valley Road. About 1 mile from ID 75, the road becomes Trail Creek Road/NFD 51. Site A is about 4.7 miles from Ketchum, where Trail Creek flattens out and creates nice gravel bars. Site B is about 11 miles from Ketchum, or 1.5 miles below Trail Creek Summit if you have to backtrack. There is a stretch of about 0.4 mile of the slate that ends at Site B. To reach Site C, drive up the hill about 14.2 miles from Ketchum, then turn left onto Little Fall Creek Road. To reach Site D, drive 16.2 miles east from Ketchum and turn right onto Phi Kappa Creek Road. Drive past the old mill remains and the surrounding camp for about 1.4 miles. The road takes you right to the main Phi Kappa Mine, though there are additional adits in the area. Note: On one visit up here, a loaded semi came barreling down the mountain, probably thinking it would be a shortcut from US 93 to ID 75. His brakes were smoking when he rolled past us.

Rockhounding

The gravels along Trail Creek at Site A are fairly typical, featuring mostly quartz, granite, and metamorphic rocks. For some rockhounds, that may be all their vehicle will allow. Site B is a well-known graptolite locale, found in Ordovician-Silurian shale. The little fossils appear as white marks against the dark rock, but they're elusive. I also found molds of wormlike critters. Be sure to park very carefully here, and don't let debris fall on the road. As you get closer to the coordinates, look for the thin slate. Be prepared to split a lot of pieces, and good luck—there seem to be only traces.

Site C contains small and perfect little quartz crystals, some of striking brilliance under a lens; there are more as you go up this road, but it's treacherous in places. There is a nice little camping area that also serves as a turn-around where the road more or less fords the creek, though I was worried about puncturing my tires. I found some very strange agate here at the camp,

Drusy quartz from Site C, showing small, stubby quartz crystals

which looked totally out of place. Sometimes rockhounds empty their rock bags in strange places. My GPS reading is a camping spot about 0.8 mile in, and I found all that I needed near there. (Ream reports more small quartz crystals farther in, plus molybdenite, and Fisher has the GPS readings; see bibliography.) The very rough road crosses the creek and proceeds about 2.5 miles from Trail Creek Road to a fork, with the molybdenum prospect about 0.6 mile to the left. There are reports of a prospect with molybdenite, tungsten, silver, and gold up Big Falls Road/NFD 168.

Site D is the old Phi Kappa Mine, which is situated in a skarn and worked a big quartz vein with sulfides such as galena, sphalerite, pyrite, and chalcopyrite. That's another rough road, so be advised. There are numerous decaying buildings in the flats.

80. East Fork Salmon River

See map on page 220.
Land type: Rolling sagebrush hills, basalt cliffs
County: Custer
GPS: A: 44.26711, -114.32593; 5,366 feet (river)
   B: 44.22422, -114.27340; 5,765 feet (Spar Canyon)
   C: 44.17979, -114.21845; 6,126 feet (Road Creek)
   D: 44.13868, -114.28098; 5,952 feet (Herd Creek)
Best season: Spring through fall

Giant gypsum boulder from Squaw Canyon

Land manager: BLM–Challis

Material: Quartz, agate, jasper, opal, opalized and petrified wood, drusy quartz, gypsum

Tools: Geology pick

Vehicle: Any; roads are gravel but very good.

Accommodations: Developed campsites at Little Boulder Creek; single site at Herd Lake; open BLM lands for primitive camping (avoid private land)

Special attractions: Salmon River Scenic Byway; Herd Lake

Finding the site: From Clayton (barely a wide spot in the road on ID 75, about 24 miles southwest of Challis), drive east on ID 75 about 4.2 miles, paralleling the Salmon River. Swing right onto East Fork Road, which now parallels the East Fork of the Salmon River. There is a lot of private land down here, but as soon as you make the turn, look for a small turnoff to the left along the East Fork. This is Site A, which provides access to decent accumulations of gravels. There is a nice park on the other side of the highway.

To reach Site B, drive about 4.2 miles up East Fork Road. Look for the turn to Spar Canyon, off to the left, and drive about 0.5 mile to Site B. To reach Site C, drive about 6.8 miles on East Fork Road from ID 75 and turn left onto Road Creek Road. Continue about 3.8 miles. To reach Site D, drive 9.1 miles on East Fork Road from its intersection with ID 75. Look for a left turn onto Herd Creek Road and drive up Herd Creek about 1.7 miles.

Rockhounding

This is a great area, and has been a staple in rockhounding literature dating back to Beckwith, Beste, Johnson, etc. The material runs large in spots, but many areas near the road are picked clean, so leave yourself some time to wander the hills. Try to time your visit so that you aren't on a southern exposure during the heat of summer.

Site A is a "quickie" spot if you don't have time to get much beyond the pavement. You won't find a lot of fresh material, but there is enough here to convince you that the hills above are productive. Site B in Spar Canyon offered the best jasper I found around here, plus quartz, agate, and a nice bit of drusy material with small, sparkly quartz crystals. The term "spar" refers to gypsum, calcite, or aragonite forming stacked crystals and displaying a satiny luster. See if you can find some of the spar material that gave the canyon its name. Basically, check every white vein you can spot.

Assorted material from Herd and Road Creeks

Site C on Road Creek features red and blue agate, some nice banded agate, and an interesting variety of geodes with coarse quartz crystals inside. If you find anything about softball-size and fairly round, you might want to bring it home and cut it rather than bash it with a hammer. Site D on Herd Creek features a nice agate, milky and blue, with some red. Park and search all the way down the hill to the creek to locate even more material in the limited creek gravels. I'm sure hiking around the hills out here would yield bigger material.

It would take at least a week to completely explore this part of Idaho. In addition to the great collecting along the East Fork, we also drove up Squaw Creek, about 7 miles west of Site A, and located Cinnabar Creek. The material in that drainage was also excellent, but there is an active mine up Squaw Creek with a lot of truck traffic. Fisher (see bibliography) shows a trilobite locale right where the trucks come barreling down the hill.

81. Bayhorse

See map on page 220.

Land type: Sagebrush hills
County: Custer
GPS: A: 44.39151, -114.29410; 5,755 feet (creek)
　　　B: 44.39742, -114.31437; 6,125 feet (mill)
　　　C: 44.39899, -114.32234; 6,363 feet (kilns)
Best season: Summer
Land manager: USDA Forest Service–Challis National Forest; Idaho State Parks
Material: Gold, garnet schist, quartz
Tools: Gold-panning equipment, geology pick
Vehicle: Any
Accommodations: This new site is a recent addition to the Land of the Yankee Fork State Park, a day-use area. Developed campground at Bayhorse Lake; primitive camping above here on national forest lands.
Special attractions: Salmon River Scenic Byway; Custer Motorway; open-air mining museum south of Challis; Challis Hot Springs resort
Finding the site: From Challis, head south on US 93 for 2.5 miles; turn right (east) onto ID 75. Drive 8.7 miles to the turn for Bayhorse Creek Road, then cross the creek and follow the signs upstream. About 2.2 miles up the road, note the small dirt track leading down the hill at a sharp angle to the left. Site A is at the creek crossing. About 1.3 miles farther, Site B offers a view of the mill. Site C is about 3.8 miles from ID 75 and features a thin garnet-bearing phyllite near the charcoal kilns.

Rockhounding

We panned at the creek crossing and picked out ore samples and tumbler material from the cold, clear water. I found good quartz, some nice garnets, black sand, and a little color in just a few minutes' panning. Don't do anything to disrupt this creek crossing—dig below or above the ford.

Up near the charcoal kilns, I found a road cut with impossibly thin schist—more likely, phyllite—with tiny garnets dispersed throughout. There is access to more of the mines in this area; a particular kind of silver ore, ramshorn, is so named because of the spectacular curling effect it has when forming a large mass. Ramshorn Mountain overlooks Bayhorse, and the Ramshorn Mine is

Large tailings pile above Bayhorse Lake

The old mill at Bayhorse Lake is a prominent landmark in this district.

at the end of NFD 381, up Bayhorse Creek off NFD 051. Meanwhile, the buildings are photo friendly, and it's an easy drive to a nice ghost town, with some decent rockhounding thrown in.

82. Yankee Fork

See map on page 220.
Land type: Dredge tailings, riverbed
County: Custer
GPS: A: 44.33540, -114.72134; 6,218 feet (bridge)
     B: 44.37694, -114.72297; 6,389 feet (dredge)
     C: 44.38933, -114.69354; 6,511 feet (Custer)
Best season: Summer; low water is best.
Land manager: USDA Forest Service–Challis National Forest
Material: Gold; some quartz and old metamorphic rocks in tailings
Tools: Gold pan, sluice, screens, shovels; hammer
Vehicle: Any; 4WD suggested for exploring
Accommodations: Many developed campsites along lower Yankee Fork and main stem of the Salmon River; primitive camping throughout on national forest lands
Special attractions: Salmon River Scenic Byway. Yankee Fork gold dredge and Custer museum are family-friendly and wheelchair accessible.
Finding the site: From Sunbeam on ID 75, drive north on Yankee Fork Road about 5.5 miles to the bridge; this is Site A. Site B is the big Yankee Fork gold dredge, about 8.7 miles from ID 75. Site C, 10.2 miles from ID 75, is the ghost town/mining camp of Custer, with photogenic old buildings and a great museum.

Rockhounding

This is a great area for exploring, even if you're armed with little more than a gold pan and hand trowel. I found interesting quartz throughout the tailings piles, and there are sulfides inside some of the quartz cobbles if you break them up. I mostly found pyrite, plus a little galena.

Geologically, this area's bedrock consists of Paleozoic and Mesozoic rock intruded by granite of the Idaho Batholith. Typical quartz vein material is fine-grained, coarse comb, or drusy. Ore minerals include an amazing variety of pyrite and silver-related ores, such as chalcopyrite, sphalerite, tetrahedrite, galena, argentite, and electrum.

The bridge locale at Site A is an easy spot for panning, but it's not the only one. Any area you find that sits on an inside bend and is reasonably easy to reach should give you ample black sands and fine flour gold. Nuggets and flakes take a lot more earth-moving, but the farther from the road you get,

Yankee Fork dredge is open for tours.

the more likely you'll have luck. Even though the dredge turned this valley upside down, there are still active claims throughout, and only the easiest gold is gone. Subsequent floods and high water have kept this small fork of the Salmon River interesting.

There are many side roads to explore as well while looking for rusty staining among quartz veins. Plus that big dredge didn't make it up small waterways like Ramey and Rankin Creeks. If you have time, try getting off the beaten track a little and sampling some of those smaller runs. You might even stumble upon a smaller mine with good tailings and locate some nice galena or silver ore.

Be sure to stop at Bonanza City, the big dredge, and the remains of Custer. These towns were part of the Wild West at one time, but it takes a vivid imagination to "see" thousands of miners prowling those old dusty streets. If you take a left turn at the dredge and drive up Loon Creek, you'll find a large open-pit mine and the Loon Creek summit; after about 21 miles, you'll see Grouse Creek Road. This was the site of the old Casto Mining District, and you should be able to recover fine gold here as well.

83. Napias Creek

See map on page 220.

Land type: Creek banks in alpine forest

County: Lemhi

GPS: A: 45.17061, -114.15734; 6,070 feet (camp, creek access)
   B: 45.22386, -114.11329; 6,646 feet (Leesburg)

Best season: Late summer; need low water

Land manager: USDA Forest Service–Salmon-Challis National Forest

Material: Petrified wood, agate, opal, jasper; placer gold and black sands

Tools: Geology pick, gold-panning equipment

Vehicle: Sturdy 4WD with good tires and strong suspension required

Accommodations: Primitive camping at site; developed camping along Panther Creek

Special attractions: Salmon River Scenic Byway; Shoup ghost town; Panther Creek Hot Springs; falls along Napias Creek; Native American pictographs along the Salmon River

Finding the site: From Shoup, drive west on Salmon River Road/NFD 30 for 8.3 miles, then turn left onto NFD 55/Panther Creek Road. Drive 18.8 miles, then turn left onto Napias Creek Road/NFD 201. After 2.9 miles continue on NFD 242 for 1.5 miles to Site A, at a giant fire ring that marks a camping area on the creek. To reach Site B, at Leesburg, drive 4.7 miles up Napias Creek. Check out the gold mining history there.

If you don't want to drive all the way around via Shoup and have an epically sturdy 4WD, try heading west from Salmon on Old Leesburg Road/NFD 082 to the townsite and mine at Leesburg, then drive south about 5 miles. It is a very slow, rutted, bumpy drive.

Rockhounding

Geologists refer to this general area as either the Leesburg or Mackinaw Mining District. Gold placers at Wards Gulch on Napias Creek were soon joined by miners on Moose and Beaver Creeks. The geology of the area is a jumble of Precambrian Belt Series rocks, Ordovician Kinnikinic quartzite, Cretaceous Idaho Batholith, and Oligocene Challis volcanics. Ores are found in at least five different complexes, primarily quartz veins with pyrite, epidote, magnetite, galena, sphalerite, and specularite.

Napias Creek near Site B

Crumbling ruins at Leesburg

Site A is a pleasant creek walk, so try to time your visit for one of those warm days when you won't mind playing in the water. The gravels aren't as clean as I like, but they're still easy to identify. Look for quartz, a reasonable agate, good jasper, and large pieces of petrified wood. Try your luck gold panning here too; gravels to the north at Leesburg were quite valuable.

If you're looking for gold, check Arnett Creek and above Leesburg for more tailings. The creek passes under the road at 45.22215, -114.10824, and it should yield colors. The entire stretch of the Salmon River below Shoup witnessed dozens of placer operations over the years as well.

84. Meyers Cove

See map on page 220.

Land type: Forested pits, prospects

County: Lemhi

GPS: A: 44.84212, -114.51208; 5,344 feet (lower locale)

    B: 44.84891, -114.50443; 6,392 feet (cut)

    C: 44.85521, -114.49613; 7,131 feet (top)

Best season: Summer

Land manager: USDA Forest Service–Salmon-Challis National Forest

Material: Fluorite

Tools: Heavy hammer, chisels

Vehicle: 4WD suggested for long drive to gate

Accommodations: Primitive camping along Panther Creek; excellent campground at Meyers Cove, or try Lost Spring Campground.

Special attractions: Salmon River Scenic Byway; gateway to River of No Return Wilderness

Finding the site: From Challis, head north on US 93 about 8 miles, then turn left onto Morgan Creek Road. Continue for 28.3 miles to the left turn for Silver Creek Road. Follow this road about 13.3 miles to Meyers Cove Campground on Camas Creek Road. About 0.5 mile from the campground, you'll encounter a gate. There is ample parking here. Just past the gate, a poor road begins climbing the mountain to Fluorspar Gulch.

Rockhounding

The material here is well worth the drive to a part of Idaho that is far off the beaten track. I found one nice exposure about 0.4 mile from the gate, including a solid green specimen and another fist-size chunk displaying excellent square crystal habits. This may be the premiere fluorite collecting area in Idaho.

To reach more mines and prospects in Fluorspar Gulch, hike another 1.1 miles along the trail to a major junction. Take the left fork, up and around the opposite hillside, to find additional cuts up to, including, and past Site B, which is about 0.5 mile away. Site C is probably as far up the hill as you'll want to go; it's almost to the top at a major cut. From the turn to Site B, stay on Fluorspar Gulch Road and go about 1.7 miles, zigzagging to the top of the ridge to another major cut. It's a long way to walk.

Fluorite crystals are square and tend to show tinting of purple or green.

One problem with fluorite is its eagerness to give up some color upon exposure to the sun's rays. My best greenish sample was hacked fresh out of the hillside. With luck you can find some purple material up here, but it will probably take time to hike around the hill. There are more cuts to sample besides Sites B and C, so again, leave time for plenty of work up here and explore as much of Fluorspar Ridge as you can.

I walked many of the gravel bars along Camas Creek below the gulch and found a little tumbler material. There is plenty more along Panther Creek. There are reports of seam agate in the ash beds along Silver Creek.

More notes for this general area: About 3 miles from the turn from Morgan Creek Road for Meyers Cove, there is a poor 3-mile 4WD track to Opal Lake. Old guidebooks show a sizable fire opal locale in the area. We poked our nose up Opal Creek Road, but it was late and the road was very poor, so we didn't make the trek. Sadly, we also saved the Yellowjacket District for another day, but we did check on the Blackbird Mining District. It's gated off, and the creek is still running orange from the Blackbird Mine due to iron staining. There are amazing cobbles of quartzite in Panther Creek, by the way, and easy access along the drive to Meyers Cove before you start the final plunge.

85. Morgan Creek

See map on page 220.

Land type: Open sagebrush, steep canyons
County: Custer
GPS: A: 44.66787, -114.22956; 5,649 feet (campground)
      B: 44.66463, -114.22748; 5,520 feet (canyon)
Best season: Year-round, but avoid summer heat and winter snow.
Land manager: BLM–Challis
Material: Quartz-rich, somewhat agatized rhyolite; agate, jasper
Tools: Heavy hammer

A canyon full of quartzite at Morgan Creek

Vehicle: Any; road is gravel but in excellent condition.
Accommodations: Developed camping at Morgan Creek Campground (Site A); primitive sites to the west along NFD 057
Special attractions: Salmon River Scenic Byway; Salmon River
Finding the site: From Challis, head north on US 93 about 8 miles and swing left onto Morgan Creek Road. After about 3.4 miles, the canyon interior appears to be slightly to solidly agatized throughout. Park safely and explore this area. After 5 miles, the campground is on your left, marked by a prominent sign. If coming south from Meyers Cove, you can't miss it on your way to Challis.

Rockhounding

The Challis area is a giant caldera, as you can see from the outdoor swimming pool at Challis Hot Springs. The walls of the caldera completely encircle the small town. This spot on Morgan Creek takes you right through the ring, where the rock is agatized and hard.

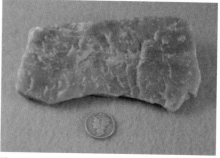

The quartzite here is hard, plentiful, and occasionally quite colorful.

The campground at Morgan Creek has a lot of agate and quartz material just lying on the surface, and if you start walking the road, you'll find more. The creek itself isn't worth checking, as too many cattle roam the hills above and the rocks are covered with green slime. But that's not a problem, as the canyon walls offer multiple opportunities for at least 2 miles. Look for white quartz seams in the reddish walls, or search the rubble under the cliffs for material you like. Some rock is uniformly reddish, while other material is banded and seamed.

At one point, we were ready to order a dump truck, as the BLM offers a community pit in this area. There are tons of rocks to bring home, and you should be able to find all you need after safely parking in the canyon. Be aware that vans and pickups zoom through here on the way to Cobalt, Meyers Cove, and other locales. Stick to the side of the road, park very carefully, and don't wander.

86. Challis

See map on page 220.
Land type: Sagebrush hills, pits and diggings
County: Custer
GPS: A: 44.48619, -114.33181; 6,772 feet (fluorite)
     B: 44.39745, -114.07394; 5,855 feet (Lime Creek)
     C: 44.37203, -114.07625; 6,038 feet (Grandview Canyon)
     D: 44.3561, -114.05549; 6,045 feet (zeolites)
     E: 44.33691, -114.03821; 6,272 feet (McGowan Creek)
Best season: Year-round, but avoid summer heat and winter snow.
Land manager: BLM–Challis
Material: Agate, fluorite, opal, jasper, petrified wood, zeolite
Tools: Geology pick; hammer and chisel/shovel for diggings
Vehicle: 4WD suggested; these side roads are a challenge.

Sagebrush flats south of Challis

Accommodations: Primitive camping on national forest lands west of here on Garden Creek Road; motels and RV parks in Challis

Special attractions: Salmon River Scenic Byway; Land of the Yankee Fork Visitor Center, just south of Challis

Finding the site: From US 93 in Challis, turn onto Main Street and drive west. Follow Main Street until it becomes Garden Creek Road/NFD 070. After 5.2 miles, turn right to stay on NFD 070. You'll see some diggings and mine ruins at Daugherty Springs, but continue up the hill almost exactly 1 mile from the turnoff. Look for a faint dirt track that leads to some pits and diggings after less than 0.25 mile. These are the fluorite pits of Site A.

To reach the rest of the Challis locales, from Challis drive south on US 93. About 10.5 miles south of the intersection with Main Street, look for Lime Creek Road and turn left. Go about 1 mile to the diggings at Site B. Site C is about 12.2 miles south of Main Street on US 93. Turn left onto a nondescript dirt track; about 0.2 mile in there is a nice gully system to explore. Site D is about 14 miles south of Main Street on US 93; the primitive road to the left isn't named. Drive about 0.3 mile. Site E is along an unmarked road about 15.5 miles south of town on US 93; if you lose track of the mileage, it's about 0.3 mile south of a major ranch on the right. Drive in about 0.7 mile east of the highway.

Rockhounding

Site A is the Garden Creek fluorite locale, offering purple and green fluorite crystals and massive fluorite. Please don't take any more than you need so that this site remains productive for a long time. The Living Waters Retreat now controls the fluorite deposit, so you might want to call ahead (208-879-2729) to check on status. There were no gates as of 2019, but that can always change. Bring a hammer and chisel, and use eye protection.

Site B is Lime Creek, with agate, petrified wood, and broken crystal-lined geodes. From the coordinates, start searching for likely spots and go up the road for at least a mile or two. Site C is more of the same, scattered in draws and gullies below Grandview Canyon. Walk the gulches for quite a distance to get off the beaten track. Site D has some impressive zeolite diggings along one prominent outcrop; some of the finest zeolites in the world have come from this draw. I also found quartz, opal, and a common rhyolite picture rock out here, but I had to do a lot of hiking. The zeolites are the main draw, however. Site E, even farther south, offered a lot of tube agate and larger pieces of banded agate, but it is getting picked over and you'll have to do more hiking

Purple fluorite seam from Site A

Representative sample from various Challis locales

there to get away from the road. Use the coordinates as a starting point, then range north to the gully, or south, or aim your vehicle straight for the ridge and follow the faint tracks to the outcrops.

Wander the hills if you have time, and pry up anything that looks good. Respect any postings and private property, but it's usually OK to open gates that aren't locked as long as you close them behind you. Beware of rattlesnakes and sharp cactus spines. If you see anyone out here, chat them up for information about land status and good collecting.

There is an excellent calcite locale at Chilly Cemetery.

87. Leaton Gulch

See map on page 220.
Land type: Desert gulch
County: Custer
GPS: 44.525397, -114.10299; 6,750 feet
Best season: Year-round, but avoid summer heat and winter snow.
Land manager: BLM–Challis
Material: Meteorite impact breccia
Tools: Geology pick and heavy hammer
Vehicle: 4WD suggested
Accommodations: Primitive camping on national forest lands west of here on Garden Creek Road; motels and RV parks in Challis
Special attractions: Challis Hot Springs
Finding the site: From Main Street in Challis, drive south on US 93 for 3.7 miles, then turn left onto Hot Springs Road. Drive 1.6 miles, stay right to remain on the main road, and drive another 1.6 miles. Turn left onto Upper Hot Springs Road and go 0.2 mile, then turn right onto NFD 111/Leaton Gulch Road. Follow it for 3.7 miles, as it gets steadily worse, to a major curve away from the creek bed. This is the start of the pink breccia.

Rockhounding

This site marks the western edge of an enormous meteorite impact crater that stretches into Montana. The Beaverhead Crater is at least 37 miles in diameter, and dates to about 600 million years, a period known as the Neoproterozoic era. The crater evidence has been studied extensively in the Beaverhead region of Montana, where shatter cones helped confirm its nature and structure in 1990. It is one of only eight known impact events on our planet with craters more than 50 km (30 miles) in diameter.

The pink quartzite is from the Middle Ordovician Kinnikinic quartzite. "Breccia" is a term for a rock created by cementing together smaller pieces that are not rounded. If the pieces were round, it would be a conglomerate. The cement that holds a breccia together is usually some kind of iron-rich or calcium-rich solution that hardened. In this case, it seems like it was heat that glued the breccia together.

Hard, prominent quartzite breccia at Leaton Gulch is the western extent of the Beaverhead impact crater.

What also isn't clear (at least to me) is whether all the breccia at this site represents part of the impact crater, such as rubble. From their stylized stratigraphic map, it sure looks like there is a thick layer of breccia stretching across the entire impact. Complicating things, there are two distinct units—an upper layer, cropping out near Grouse Peak about 1 mile to the north, and a lower layer, which begins at the coordinates. Carr and Link (1999) have unraveled a lot of the different pods and lenses of unique breccias inside the overall locale, and they report the quartzite particles, or grains (some of which are very large), show a characteristic deformation that cuts across grain boundaries. That would seem to indicate that the breccia was already in place, and then shocked by the bolide (large meteor). Some zones show grains with deformation that does not cross grain boundaries, seeming to mean they were shocked first and then welded together.

Clearly there is a lot of work to do here, including drilling core samples, which won't be easy in such hard rock. We know there has been a lot of crustal movement in the Challis area in general that has affected evidence for the impact crater. As the authors state, "Reconstruction of a dismembered Neoproterozoic meteor impact crater in an area affected by multiple superposed deformational events is chancy business." At any rate, grab some hunks of the bottom of the breccia, or download their paper and investigate further on your own.

Pink quartzite breccia from the lower unit

88. Lemhi Pass

See map on page 242.
Land type: Alpine forest, tailings, creek bed
County: Lemhi
GPS: A: 44.97280, -113.48176; 5,915 feet (placer)
   B: 44.96879, -113.47509; 6,334 feet (mine)
Best season: Mid-July through September; snow can block the pass through July.
Land manager: USDA Forest Service–Salmon-Challis National Forest
Material: Malachite, placer gold; black sands rich in thorium
Tools: Gold-panning equipment, big hammer
Vehicle: 4WD suggested for the short drive to mine
Accommodations: Excellent camping at Agency Creek Recreation Site; lots of primitive camping on national forest lands near Lemhi Pass
Special attractions: Lewis and Clark Back Country Byway; Sacajawea Scenic Byway; Sacajawea Memorial Camp at Lemhi Pass; Fort Lemhi Monument
Finding the site: From the Tendoy store on ID 28, go east 0.2 mile on Tendoy Lane, then turn right onto Old Highway 28. After heading south 0.3 mile, turn left onto the Lewis and Clark Byway, which follows Agency Creek for 9.1 miles. You'll pass the campground first, then the old Red Rock Stage Stop, and finally reach a warning sign about "Gold panning only." These are the placer tailings at Site A. A

Decaying old cabin near Site B

Site 88

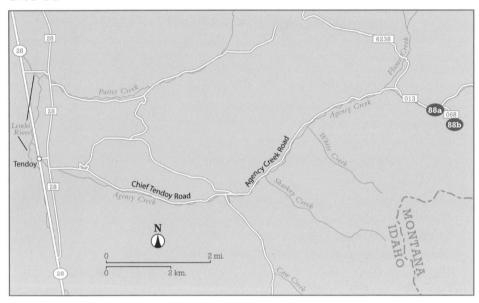

right turn up the hill takes you to the old mine ruins in only 0.4 mile. This road is steep and a bit bumpy, so if you have a passenger car, you may want to park and walk to Site B.

Rockhounding

Of all the metal mines, I like copper mines the best. Here at the Copper Queen Mine, even the lowest-grade ore has enough green malachite to simplify the search. For me, the quest is always straightforward: Green is great, but try to find some blue azurite. Malachite and azurite are usually found together, although azurite is more rare.

I found good malachite, some very bright green, and one pinpoint of azurite went into the sample bag. In addition to the showy copper minerals, try to break enough ore material to find some of the shiny metals. Given enough time and sampling, you should be able to locate bornite, a nice peacock ore, plus other rarities. Geological reports indicate the presence of gold, silver, lead, zinc, copper, cobalt, molybdenum, and thorium.

The thorium here is easy to pan in Agency Creek if you follow some simple rules. Look for a turn or trap in the creek, especially near large boulders, and screen your sample before panning. You should find loads of black sand here—but don't store it in a vial in your front pocket. As described in

Malachite from the productive dumps at Site B

Roadside Geology of Idaho (see bibliography), "According to some estimates, which are probably conservative, the reserves of thorium at Lemhi Pass are the largest known to exist in the United States. . . . Thorium is an interesting radioactive element with almost no industrial use. If a significant market for thorium should ever develop, the deposits at Lemhi Pass might someday support mines, probably open pits. Rare earth elements do have their uses, so it is possible that mines may someday produce them at Lemhi Pass, even if no demand for thorium ever materializes."

Fisher (see bibliography) shows some fossil leaf locales on Cow and Haynes Creeks, though private property may be a problem. There are a couple good road cuts to check for fossils as you drive up to the pass.

89. Spencer Opal Mines

See map on page 245.

Land type: City

County: Clark

GPS: 44.361241, -112.18621; 5,892 feet (parking lot)

Best season: May through October; mine visit by appointment only

Land manager: Private (mine); USDA Forest Service–Caribou-Targhee National Forest

Material: Precious opal—the kind with the little pins of fire that can be mesmerizing

Tools: Credit card if buying from the shops. If working the fee area, heavy crack hammer, spray bottle, safety glasses, bucket, chisels, gloves, long pants, and boots—no open-toed shoes allowed.

Vehicle: Any

Accommodations: None at site; developed campground 3 miles north at Stoddard Creek; RV park in Spencer; motels in Dubois

Special attractions: Fort Henry Historic Byway; Lost Gold Trails Loop; Fort Harkness, near Humphrey; Bannack Pass

Finding the site: Exit I-15 at Spencer, then follow the signs on Opal Avenue to the Opal Country Cafe, which is also the showroom and mine headquarters. You are roughly 65 miles north of Idaho Falls, 70 miles west of Yellowstone National Park, and 80 miles south of Dillon, Montana.

Storefront for one of the leading opal vendors in Spencer

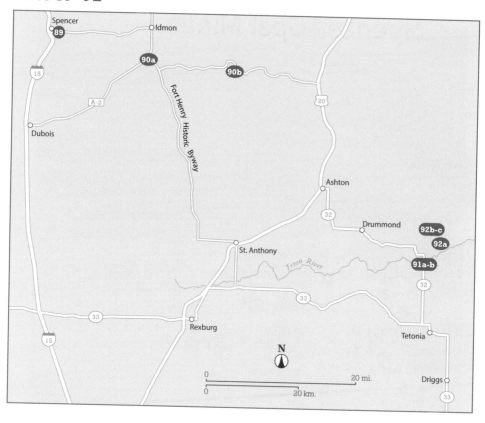

Rockhounding

This is a fee-dig operation. The on-site tailings are available roughly from Memorial Day through the end of September, but the mine diggings are greatly restricted. In recent years, the diggings were open only thirteen days during the entire summer season. This means that you must plan ahead, make reservations, and keep them. Check at spenceropalmines.com.

The mine will also consider group reservations, so if you want to organize an outing for up to twenty members of your local rock club, you could go that route.

The cafe offers good food and a nice rock shop full of material to bring home. I picked up a couple of precious opal pendants for an excellent price. These are the famed "triplets"—a true lapidary feat. Jewelers glue a slab of thin precious opal on top of a dark material, such as obsidian or black basanite, which brings out the play of color to the greatest intensity. Since opal is very soft, this "doublet" is then covered with a clear quartz layer to make a protective triplet.

Inexpensive opal jewelry from Spencer

Several other shops in Spencer sell rough and finished precious opal. If you're in the mood for a little shopping, look for their signs and drop in to see what kind of deals you can make. We checked out Hopper on Old Highway 91, a short distance south from Spencer, and were wowed. There are lots of options; once you're in town, you'll have no trouble spotting which businesses are in the opal trade.

90. Cinder Butte

See map on page 245.

Land type: Desert sagebrush

County: Clark

GPS: A: 44.31090, -111.92050; 6,316 feet (old pits)

B: 44.28977, -111.69267; 6,819 feet (new locale)

Best season: Year-round, but avoid hot part of day in summer.

Land manager: BLM–Upper Snake

Material: Sunstones, plus unusual lava forms

Tools: Geology pick

Vehicle: Any; road is paved from St. Anthony to Site A, so you could park safely and hike to the butte if you had to. Site B leans to 4WD toward the end.

Accommodations: Primitive camping on BLM lands; developed campground north on Camas Creek

Special attractions: Fort Henry Historic Byway; Lost Gold Trails Loop; Island Park Reservoir

Finding the site: From Bridge Street in St. Anthony, turn left onto Fourth Street North and follow it west as it becomes East 600 North. After about 4.7 miles, swing right (north) onto Salem Road/Red Road. Drive past the dunes area, skip the immense cinder deposit off to the left, and follow Red Road for about 27 miles.

Bad news at the old pit

Hook up with CR A-2, coming in from the west. To reach Site B, leave US 20 east of St. Anthony on Yellowstone Highway, and drive north, then west 0.8 mile, across the bridge. Turn right onto Yellowstone Highway and drive just 0.2 mile, then continue on Sand Creek Road. Drive 15.5 miles, then turn left onto Red Sand Creek Bed Road and drive 5 miles. Take a slight right, and drive 4.1 miles to take a left onto Davis Lake Road. Drive 1.6 miles, then turn left and go about 0.4 mile to the parking area.

Rockhounding

Sunstones are a variety of feldspar, sometimes called andesine, and they will facet nicely if solid. They are thus highly sought, but in 2019 the main pit used by rockhounds for years was closed. Visit clark-co.id.gov/county-officials and then call someone to complain; maybe you can do better than I did.

At Site B, you'll need to climb the ridge to get to the boulders at the top that contain the sunstones. Not many have eroded out, so consider grabbing some hand specimens and breaking them up carefully at home.

Don't think about taking a shortcut across the ranchland to move from Site A to Site B. The roads are barely visible at many points, and it's very slow going.

Small sunstone fragments are still available at the new coordinates, but they're not as plentiful.

91. Bitch Creek

See map on page 245.
Land type: Large stream with limited forest
County: Fremont-Teton line
GPS: A: 43.93614, -111.17808; 5,925 feet (parking)
B: 43.93987, -111.17928; 5,840 feet (bridge)
Best season: Late summer for lowest possible water
Land manager: Idaho Fish and Wildlife
Material: Jade; agate, jasper, and other tumbler material
Tools: Heavy hammer; pocketknife for field scratch test on jade
Vehicle: Any; roads are paved to parking area.
Accommodations: None at site; primitive camping on extensive national forest lands to the east, all the way to the Wyoming border and on Conant Creek; two national parks with developed campgrounds farther east
Special attractions: Mesa Falls Scenic Byway; Teton Scenic Byway; Grand Teton National Park; Yellowstone National Park
Finding the site: From Ashton on US 20, drive southeast 21.1 miles on ID 32 to the south parking site, with access down to the creek. To reach Site B, go north across the bridge, just a short distance away.

Bitch Creek from Site B

Rockhounding

Back in the day, rockhounds had many more access points to both Bitch Creek and its important tributary, Tetonia Jade Creek. Over the years, however, new landholders have taken over the old ranches and blocked most corridors to the creek. This spot remains open for fishing access, though it's a hike from the parking area down to the creek. And being the easiest access point, this spot is hit hard.

Slice of jade from Bitch Creek

Another locale is an outcrop on the other side of the bridge. While looking for tiny quartz crystals in an ash deposit there, I noticed some cobbles and pebbles that looked a lot like jade. Figuring they could have been deposited by Bitch Creek long ago, I took them home, and one of them appeared to test out.

Jade is a notoriously difficult specimen to identify in the field, and Idaho jade is no different. Some material may occur as a dark green—almost black—cobble or pebble, polished smooth with few, if any, chips or gouges. Some is closer to whitish green.

Jade sometimes forms a white or rusty orange rind if it weathers for long periods. This weathered material is considerably softer than unaltered jade, so the common pocketknife test can steer you wrong. Ordinarily, a steel pocketknife cannot scratch jade. Another test is to knock off a corner and hold it to the sun to test for translucence. This assumes you have a strong enough hammer to actually break off a chunk of jade. Keep in mind that all over the world, early man would lash a solid hunk of jade to the end of a forked stick to use as a club, and the stick and lashings would break long before the jade would splinter. Most likely, if you can break off a corner to test it, it probably isn't jade.

My best suggestion is to check with a local expert before heading to the creek. About 24 miles south of the Bitch Creek site is the lively town of Driggs, home of the Teton Jade and Gem shop at 140 North Main. The shop is also the primary plumbing supply store for miles around, which ensures that owner David Driggs opens for business early in the morning. He has samples of Idaho jade for purchase that will help you sharpen your eye, and he can steer you toward other local hot spots, including fossils along Pine Creek Pass and the mining district at Packsaddle Basin.

92. Conant Creek

See map on page 245.
Land type: Creek beds, open forest
County: Fremont
GPS: A: 44.00466, -111.15049; 5,822 feet (creek)
    B: 44.00439, -111.15352; 5,793 feet (creek)
    C: 43.98172, -111.13558; 6,259 feet (dry gulch)
Best season: Late summer for low water
Land manager: USDA Forest Service–Caribou-Targhee National Forest
Material: Agate, jasper, petrified wood, gneiss, schist, granite
Tools: Geology pick
Vehicle: 4WD suggested; some bumpy gravel roads
Accommodations: Primitive camping throughout the area on national forest lands all the way to the Wyoming border (and beyond); watch for private land.
Special attractions: Mesa Falls Scenic Byway; Teton Scenic Byway; Falls River; Teton River
Finding the site: From Ashton on US 20, follow ID 32 southeast for 17.4 miles. At North 4700 East, turn off and continue for 1 mile. At Coyote Meadows Road, turn right and drive 3 miles. Turn left onto Conant–Fall River Road/NFD 263 and drive for 1.6 miles. You should see the creek off to your left. There is a fork with easy parking.

Rockhounding

On a hot August day, the first two sites are a pleasant creek walk for as long as you care to wander. The water is clear and cool, and the material is clean and piled high. You should begin to find excellent material in no time, as the creek has sorted gravels in all significant turns. There are occasional deep spots, but if the day permits, use a flotation device, wear sandals and swimming trunks, and bring a big collection bag. You should be rewarded with a nice haul. Sites A and B are close to each other and offer excellent material.

Try keeping the sun in front of you so that agates and clear quartz jump out. The jasper here is usually tan and very hard, and takes a nice polish; the wood, while scarce, is usually hard enough to cut. The USDA Forest Service boundary is about 0.5 mile west, so respect that. You can walk east for a long way, but here where the road meets the creek seemed to have the best piles

The Grand Tetons overlook the drive to Conant Creek.

Adequate gravels, good camping, and cool shade make this a decent stop before traveling on to Wyoming's Yellowstone National Park.

of gravel for searching. If you get here during high water, there are patches of gravel along the road.

If you spend time in this area, try driving Coyote Meadows Road all the way to the Wyoming border. We found nice jasper and quartz along the route in the small dry streams that meander through the meadows. This is Site C, and it seemed as though it hadn't been searched in quite a while, because we found nice pieces of jasper—some big enough to slab—at just about every stop. We also found a spot along the Teton River, coming in from the north between Drummond and Lamont.

93. Caribou Mountain

See map on page 254.

Land type: Alpine meadows, creek beds, forest

County: Bonneville

GPS: A: 43.13981, -111.34154; 6,601 feet (Barnes Creek)

      B: 43.11321, -111.27123; 6,825 feet (Anderson Creek)

      C: 43.14765, -111.24782; 6,106 feet (McCoy Creek/Iowa Creek)

      D: 43.10401, -111.26323; 6,866 feet (townsite)

Best season: Late summer

Land manager: USDA Forest Service–Caribou-Targhee National Forest

Material: Gold; creek gravels contain some quartz and jasper

Tools: Gold-panning equipment, geology pick

Vehicle: 4WD suggested; required if trying to reach Caribou City

Accommodations: Primitive camping throughout the area on extensive national forest lands; developed campgrounds at Palisades Reservoir, to the east

Special attractions: Pioneer Historic Byway; Palisades Reservoir

Stairs leading up to the tailings and information displays at Caribou City

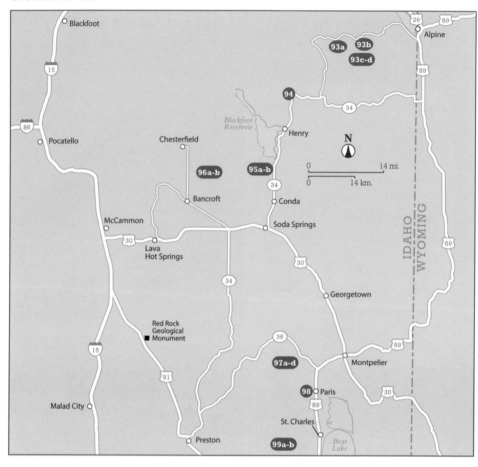

Finding the site: From Soda Springs, head north on ID 34 for 27.2 miles. Near Pelican Point, turn left (north) onto West Side Road and follow it 9 miles to Grays Lake Road. Turn right onto Grays Lake Road and continue 3.6 miles, then swing left onto NFD 087. Take this good gravel road 5.2 miles until you see the "Gold Panning Only" signs. The next right is onto NFD 188, which is Barnes Creek Road. There is good panning at the creek here; this is Site A. According to the map, the road continues all the way up to the ghost town of Keenan City.

To reach Site B, continue on NFD 087 another 5.1 miles from the Barnes Creek/NFD 188 turnoff. This is the turn for Caribou City. We ran into road construction and were unable to make it the last 1.5 miles to the old ghost town site, but Anderson Creek is a reasonable panning area. The tumbler material here is mostly quartz. To get to Site C, continue on NFD 087 about 1 mile past the turnoff for

Caribou City and look for the bridge across Iowa Creek. There are great gravel bars and panning sites upstream from the bridge on Iowa Creek, and the tumbler material here is fantastic. To reach Site D, return to the turn for Caribou City and take it. This is NFD 165. Drive 3.3 miles to the top, take a sharp left, and drive 0.3 mile more to the information kiosks at the ghost town site.

Rockhounding

Caribou City (or, properly, Cariboo City, as it was named by a veteran of the Cariboo Mining District in British Columbia) was a decent gold-mining district in its day, known as the Mount Pisgah District. It attracted thousands of miners, who dredged up a storm along lower McCoy Creek. Iowa Creek was also very busy, and there are good black sands and colors left. Most of the creeks in this area also carry good tumbler material, primarily quartz and jasper.

Forest service regulations currently restrict dredging and sluicing, so check in with the local ranger to get an update on the rules unless you just plan to pan. Don't be surprised to know more about the mining up here than the rangers do. You still should touch base, however, to see if there are any new construction projects or road changes. I did see some new claim markers close to Site D, so maybe the gold is pretty good here. You should be fine panning at the other three coordinates listed here, but be vigilant for claim markers anyway. At Site D, at the top, you can check the tailings piles at will. There is quartz in the dredge tailings, and you might find some low-grade metal ore in the lode mine tailings piled up near the stairs.

The geology of the district is described as Mesozoic country rocks intruded by dioritic sills and dikes. The ores show up in large quartz masses associated with calcite, pyrite, and gold. The quartz veins worked as lode mines were high up the mountain, above Caribou City and Keenan City. Check a topo map of the area for exact locations. Expect some long, arduous hikes to reach these relics; I've never made it to the Monte Cristo Mine, but I hear it's quite a slog.

After leaving Caribou Mountain, we took Long Valley Road toward Blackfoot and stopped at Pole Bridge, where the road crosses Willow Creek. This spot has been mentioned for years as a Tempskya (an extinct treelike fern) fossil site, but it can probably be crossed off the list. The surrounding area is fenced and off-limits. I waded around in the creek for a while, but it was smelly and slimy, and I felt like I needed a shower afterward. Plus, I didn't find anything but a few slivers of jasper.

94. Pelican Point

See map on page 254.

Land type: Large limestone quarry, big outcrop along road
County: Caribou
GPS: 43.01191, -111.51829; 6,390 feet (Pelican Point)
Best season: Spring (depending on snow) through summer
Land manager: BLM–Pocatello; USDA Forest Service–Caribou-Targhee National Forest
Material: Limestone fossils
Tools: Hammer, chisels
Vehicle: Any for Pelican Point if you park; Henry Cutoff is graveled and bumpy.
Accommodations: Developed camping on Gravel Creek; primitive camping on national forest lands throughout the area
Special attractions: Pioneer Historic Byway; Oregon Trail Bear Lake Scenic Byway; Blackfoot Reservoir

You should have no trouble locating this large limestone quarry at Pelican Point.

Finding the site: From Soda Springs, drive north on ID 34 about 27 miles. The road takes a big swing here, but the Pelican Point quarry is visible off to the left. Drive about 0.4 mile to the quarry itself and begin searching.

Rockhounding

This is one of the easier limestone fossil locales to search. I had good success here, with horn corals and brachiopods the main trophies. It takes a bit of time to get your eye adjusted to looking for evidence of past life in the vast gray exposures, but have patience. If you're lucky, you might find a horn coral that is completely eroded out of the limestone matrix. They look like a little fossilized tornado.

The area around here, especially near Wayan, is extensively documented in paleontology literature. There's a great story about an amateur collector who recovered tons of Cretaceous vertebrate fossils from the area, but of course you need a permit for such activity. In addition, the older literature mentions Tempskya (treelike fern) deposits east of Wayan. I cruised through the area with a good idea about where to look, but it appeared that all the likely hillsides were now private land and off-limits. Time and time again I ran into fences and locked gates. You're going to need to befriend a local land-owner to do any serious Tempskya searching. This limestone locale is open, and the limestone outcrop nearby at Henry Cutoff (42.94723, -111.42050) is also good.

Fossilized horn coral, from the side (like a tooth) and from the top (round)

95. China Hat

See map on page 254.
Land type: Road cut
County: Caribou
GPS: A: 42.81914, -111.59965; 6,137 feet (gate)
B: 42.81515, -111.60298; 6,132 feet (road cut)
Best season: Spring through fall, maybe longer
Land manager: Private and county road right-of-way
Material: Fluorescent minerals
Tools: Hammer, chisels
Vehicle: Any
Accommodations: Developed camping near Wayan; dispersed camping on Caribou-Targhee National Forest land, to the east
Special attractions: Pioneer Historic Byway; Oregon Trail Bear Lake Scenic Byway; Montpelier Reservoir; Bear Lake; Oregon Trail Center in Montpelier

Bring a UV light to check the minerals here.

Finding the site: From Soda Springs, drive north on Main Street to ID 34 East/ Hooper Avenue for 11.5 miles. Turn left onto China Cap Road, drive 1.5 miles, then right onto Dike Road. Follow it for 0.5 mile and turn into the gated entrance to the old quarry. By custom this site has been open for rockhounding in the past, but if that has changed, or you just don't want to risk it, go to Site B. Instead of turning off China Cap Road onto Dike Road, continue another 0.5 mile to the white outcrops.

Rockhounding

Collect interesting fluorescent material, a glassy rhyolite, at this locale. Under long-wave UV light, you should see light to strong orange color. You may see streaks, solid color, or spots.

Under UV light, the electrons in an atom's outer shell are energized to the next level, and this agitated state results in different colors than those seen in normal light. Some mineral collectors specialize in fluorescents, and collect by color. By far the most famous locale for fluorescent minerals in the United States is at Sterling Hill, New Jersey, where an old zinc mine in a carbonate-rich environment is known to host more than eighty different fluorescent minerals. If you ever get a chance, go there!

It's handy to pack a portable UV light for safety reasons too. For example, scorpions fluoresce because of the calcium in their exoskeleton. You can use the UV light to help distinguish calcite from quartz too.

96. Little Flat

See map on page 254.

Land type: Sagebrush-covered rangeland
County: Caribou
GPS: A: 42.80819, -111.82596; 5,733 feet (travertine)
B: 42.81137, -111.81277; 5,878 feet (coral)
Best season: Year-round; avoid snow and hot summer days.
Land manager: BLM–Pocatello
Material: Fossil coral in limestone
Tools: Heavy hammer, chisels
Vehicle: 4WD suggested; dirt road for final approach
Accommodations: None at site; primitive camping on Pebble Creek Road, to the west. Lava Hot Springs Resort on US 30, east of McCammon, is a popular, family-friendly locale.
Special attractions: Pioneer Historic Byway; Oregon Trail Bear Lake Scenic Byway; Lava Hot Springs Resort; Soda Springs; Sulphur Springs
Finding the site: From Bancroft on Old US 30, head north on Main Street/ Chesterfield Road. Drive 6.1 miles north to the intersection with Hatch Loop Road and turn right (east). After about 1.5 miles, notice the picturesque old Hatch School. Keep driving due east as the road becomes Little Flat Road, about 2 miles after turning off Chesterfield Road. About 3.7 miles from that turn, the road will have curved up and around the travertine locale at Site A and reached a gate. Let yourself through, close the gate behind you, and proceed about 0.25 mile to the limestone outcrop ahead and to your left. This is Site B.

Rockhounding

These rocks are easy to search for life-forms, especially the spiral horn coral that shows up so readily in cross section. The fossils at Little Flat are Mississippian in age, and thus not very complex. Limestone fossils are typically difficult to break out of the host matrix, and I usually leave them in the rock and bring home big specimens.

Feel free to roam the hills in search of more material, but I've found that once I find a good horizon, it tends to stay good. There are rattlesnakes in this area, so don't lose focus of the many potential dangers. Also, my socks tended to fill up with seedpods and clusters, so I strongly recommend high-top boots.

Travertine outcrop; it's too crumbly to do much with but good to know about.

The travertine locale at Site A is not high-quality, but the formation gave Little Flat its name, so I listed it. I liked the travertine at Soda Springs better, but I wasn't about to start chipping away in the middle of a city park.

Consult the road log (Fortsch and Link, "Regional Geology and Fossil Sites, Southeastern Idaho and Western Wyoming"; see appendix A) published for this area for more fossil-hunting ideas. There are calcite mines, lime quarries, and other geological treasures to locate. I looked near Lava Hot Springs for manganese deposits, but they appeared to be on private land. The local rockhounds told me that they sometimes find arrowheads and projectile points out in the lava fields, because Indians often drove buffalo into the perilous badlands as a hunting technique. For you history buffs, the Oregon Trail came through this area en route from Soda Springs westward. Ream (see bibliography) lists a fluorescent rhyolite locale up at China Cap.

Certain zones in the limestone teem with life. This cross section of a horn coral dates to the Permian.

97. Spence Gulch

See map on page 254.
Land type: Creek bed, alpine forest, sagebrush hills
County: Bear Lake
GPS: A: 42.31153, -111.45020; 5,991 feet (Liberty)
  B: 42.29665, -111.50641; 6,989 feet (road, creek bed)
  C: 42.30333, -111.50929; 6,877 feet (gulch)
  D: 42.30284, -111.51041; 6,963 feet (camp)
Best season: Summer
Land manager: USDA Forest Service–Caribou-Targhee National Forest
Material: Ammonites, dendritic psilomelane, trilobites, black agate, quartzite, jasper
Tools: Geology pick, chisels, hammer
Vehicle: 4WD strongly suggested

Outcrop at Spence Gulch. Start by digging where someone else put in a lot of work. If you find something, stay on that level.

Accommodations: Primitive camping throughout the area on national forest lands, especially at Site D; developed sites at Emigration Campground on ID 36 east of Liberty

Special attractions: Pioneer Historic Byway; Oregon Trail Bear Lake Scenic Byway. More fossil hunting south of here in Hillyard Canyon, Cub Basin, and Franklin Basin; see Fisher (listed in the bibliography) and the US and Canada fossil site database (listed in appendix A).

Finding the site: From Liberty on ID 36, head south on Lanark Road about 0.4 mile. Site A is a large tan road cut on the west side of the road with abundant rock to split. To reach the rest of the sites, continue on Lanark Road for 0.9 mile to NFD 405/Mill Farm Road (which eventually becomes Mill Canyon Road) and turn right (west). Stay on this road for about 4.4 miles until you reach Danish Flat. A rough, unmarked road splits the valley; take a right turn onto it and go north. After about 0.5 mile, notice the abundant shale outcrops along the creek, which are barely fossiliferous here. This is Site B. There is agate and jasper in the creek gravels. If you have GPS, drive about 0.4 mile farther, or 0.9 mile from the turnoff from NFD 405, then park and make your way to the right through the brush to the trilobite locale at Spence Gulch, which is Site C. The hike is less than 0.1 mile, but there are a lot of different trails in here, so use the coordinates to head straight down the hill. Or, to be safe your first time, just hike north along the creek bed from Site B. Site D is about 1.3 miles from NFD 405 and offers good camping plus more creek gravels to explore for agate and quartzite.

Rockhounding

Site A offers some good ammonites, mostly as molds, plus nice black manganese that occurs as branchlike dendrites. Split the shale for fresh material. Site B is a good gravel area along the creek bed and also in the road. The drive here is quite rough, and you may want to just park and walk along the creek from Site B to Site C at Spence Gulch, rather than try to bushwhack from the road. You can't miss the "quarry" once you get to the creek bed, but I didn't see any way to drive to it.

Use a hammer and chisel to break up the shale and look for decent trilobites. Many varieties have come out of the quarry, so plan to spend time here and be patient and thorough. There are some papers on this locale that describe what you'll find; Charles Doolittle Walcott first collected this area in 1908. The trilobites are Middle Cambrian in age, and with luck you can find a whole specimen.

Amecephalus trilobite from Spence Gulch PHOTO COURTESY OF REBECCA HUNT-FOSTER

The camping spot at Site D is shady, with plenty of wood and a nice fire pit or two. Be very cautious if you encounter a rainy stretch here—the roads contain several "wallows" that fill up with water and are nearly impassable without the proper vehicle. I was forced to do a lot of hiking in this area, but the payoff was an attractive black agate and pleasing quartzite that I picked up as float.

98. Paris Canyon

See map on page 254.
Land type: Sagebrush hills
County: Bear Lake
GPS: 42.22436, -111.42797; 6,099 feet (ammonites)
Best season: Spring through fall
Land manager: BLM–Pocatello
Material: Ammonite fossils
Tools: Geology pick, fine-point chisels
Vehicle: Any; gravel road is in good shape
Accommodations: None at site; developed campgrounds at Paris Spring and St. Charles Canyon
Special attractions: Minnetonka Cave, Bear Lake
Finding the site: From Paris on US 89, head west on West Second Street/Paris Canyon Road. There is a sign at the turn. Drive 1.4 miles to the site, which is an extensive road cut.

This easy-to-spot road cut has decent parking and plenty of shale to split.

Rockhounding

Paris Canyon offers extensive outcrops of shale to search for ammonite impressions. These are Cretaceous fossils that resemble nautiloids—coiled-up saltwater snails, if you will. Ammonites are an interesting group of critters, and their shells sometimes contain spines or bumps.

The rock here is easy to split, and fossils aren't scarce once you get into a zone. Take your time and split as much rock as you can to look for molds and impressions. The lighter material is the Langston Formation, Middle Cambrian in age; the dark black limestone is the Phosphoria Formation. Finding an entire fossil is rare here, but possible; mostly you'll see molds. Don't be too greedy—leave a few for the next collector. Park safely, and don't leave any rocks in the road. If you see a little litter, pick it up, because it's just going to get blamed on rockhounds.

Tiny coiled ammonite mold from Paris Canyon

99. St. Charles

See map on page 254.
Land type: Steep hills
County: Bear Lake
GPS: A: 42.11551, -111.44512; 6,198 feet (boundary)
   B: 42.08811, -111.51926; 7,549 feet (cave)
Best season: Summer
Land manager: USDA Forest Service–Caribou-Targhee National Forest
Material: Various limestone fossils
Tools: Hammer, chisels
Vehicle: Any; road is paved to cave
Accommodations: Three easy-to-spot developed campgrounds along Minnetonka Cave Road; primitive camping on national forest lands
Special attractions: Pioneer Historic Byway; Oregon Trail Bear Lake Scenic Byway; tour of Minnetonka Cave
Finding the site: From St. Charles on US 89, follow Second Street west to Minnetonka Cave Road. Site A is about 3.3 miles from US 89, just after you cross the national forest boundary. The parking area at the cave (Site B) is 9.6 miles from US 89.

Rockhounding

The limestone hills in this general area are full of fossils, including brachiopods, trilobites, and horn coral. The collecting site listed here (no collecting at cave) is very general; you could set up a base camp at any of the area's fine campgrounds and conduct your own thorough exploration and probably do very well. As the literature suggests, look for red to white sandstone and blue phosphate zones. I found brachiopod and horn coral fossils throughout here. The trilobites were far more elusive than I bargained for; I hope you do better than I did.

For more information, consult the road log by Fortsch and Link, "Regional Geology and Fossil Sites, Southeastern Idaho and Western Wyoming." The report is available as an Acrobat file from the Idaho Digital Atlas (see appendix A).

By all means, make time for a tour of Minnetonka Cave. There are many fascinating cave features in this limestone marvel, including stalactites, stalagmites, and travertine. It's cool in the cave, so be sure to bring a coat or sweater,

Inside Minnetonka Cave

and leave plenty of time for the 90-minute descent. There are many fossils in the cave, but no collecting is allowed underground.

Fisher (see bibliography) lists a fossil shrimp locale along Indian Creek, across Bear Lake from St. Charles. I found more limestone fossils there, but it was the end of a long day and I lacked the energy or ambition to climb up to the top of the ridge and search the shale. Worse, when I later mentioned the site to my aunt Roberta Banta, she pointed out that nearby Garden City serves up the best raspberry milk shakes she's ever tasted. Perhaps if armed with a milk shake, I might have made it to the top of the ridge and found more than broken shells and smashed corals.

Bear Lake has a state park and extensive sandy beaches at its northern end. The blue water is a marvel in itself, so be sure to at least swing by.

There are numerous other locales nearby to search for fossils. The US and Canada fossil site database shows "abundant Cambrian fossils" in limestone and shale up Bloomington Creek Canyon, but we probably didn't go far enough. At Minnetonka Cave, there are horn corals in the rocks by the cave entrance. At Franklin Basin, we found what looked like belemnites at 42.08232, -111.62475. There are supposed to be trilobites in nearby Hillyard Canyon, and also at Two Mile Canyon near Malad City. On the Utah border at 41.99993, -111.51911, there are reports of Devonian fish fossils. Clearly, there is a lot to explore in this remote corner of Idaho.

APPENDIX A: WEBSITES

Most of these websites appear to be fairly stable, but if a link is broken, you might still be able to run a Google search and locate the entity.

Agencies, Bureaus, and Departments

Bureau of Land Management
blm.gov/id/st/en.html

Bureau of Land Management
blm.gov/idaho

Idaho Department of Lands
www.idl.idaho.gov/mining/rockhounding/index.html

Idaho Geological Survey Mines and Minerals Database
idahogeology.org/mines-minerals

Idaho Geological Survey Geology Maps
idahogeology.org/product/m-9

Idaho Scenic Byways
visitidaho.org/things-to-do/scenic-byways-backcountry-drives/

Idaho State Parks and Recreation
parksandrecreation.idaho.gov

Idaho Traffic Webcams
northwestwebcams.com/idaho-web-cams.php

Idaho Transportation Department, Traveler Information
511.idaho.gov

USDA Forest Service Links
    Boise National Forest: www.fs.fed.us/r4/boise
    Caribou-Targhee National Forest: www.fs.usda.gov/ctnf
    Clearwater National Forest: www.fs.fed.us/r1/clearwater
    Idaho Panhandle (Kaniksu) National Forests: www.fs.fed.us/ipnf
    Payette National Forest: www.fs.fed.us/r4/payette
    Salmon-Challis National Forest: www.fs.fed.us/r4/sc
    Sawtooth National Forest: www.fs.fed.us/r4/sawtooth

US Geological Survey (USGS)
usgs.gov
waterdata.usgs.gov/id/nwis/rt (water levels)

Geology and Mineralogy

Idaho Digital Atlas Geology Field Guides
digitalatlas.cose.isu.edu/geo/gsa/gsafrm.htm

Idaho Gem Guide
www.idl.idaho.gov/mining/rockhounding/gemstones.html

Idaho Obsidian Sources
sourcecatalog.com/id/s_id.html

Mineralogy Database
mindat.org

ThoughtCo.com Geology
thoughtco.com/geology-4133564

US and Canadian Fossil Sites Database
donaldkenney.x10.mx/STATES/ID.HTM

Zeolites of the World
www.mindat.org (account required; free to sign up)

Mining History

Crystal Gold Mine Tour
goldmine-idaho.com

Idaho State Historical Society Digital History Collection
idahohistory.contentdm.oclc.org/index.php

Kellogg Mining District
murray-idaho.com

Mining in Idaho
imnh.isu.edu/digitalatlas/geog/mining/minemain.htm

Murray Gold-Mining Stories
murray-idaho.com

Spencer Opal Mine
spenceropalmines.com

Museums, Schools, and Sites of Interest

Challis Bison Jump
idahoheritage.org/assets/popups/ec/ec_bison.htmlhtml

City of Rocks
nps.gov/ciro/planyourvisit/index.htm

Craters of the Moon National Monument and Preserve
nps.gov/crmo

Hagerman Horse Fossils
nps.gov/hafo/index.htm

Idaho's Great Rift
digitalatlas.cose.isu.edu/geo/greatrft/greatrft.htm

Idaho Museum of Mining and Geology
idahomuseum.org

Idaho Museum of Natural History
imnh.isu.edu

Idaho State University Geology Department
geology.isu.edu

National Register of Historic Places in Idaho
en.wikipedia.org/wiki/List_of_Registered_Historic_Places_in_Idaho

Red Rock Pass
absoluteastronomy.com/topics/Red_Rock_Pass

St. Anthony Sand Dunes
visitidaho.org/things-to-do/natural-attractions/st-anthony-sand-dunes/

University of Idaho Department of Geological Sciences
uidaho.edu/sci/geology

Wilson Butte Cave
visitsouthidaho.com/adventure/wilson-butte-cave/

Personal Web Pages

Tim Fisher's Ore-Rock-On
www.orerockon.com

Mike and Chrissy Streeter's field trips
mcrocks.com/page18.html

Rock Shops, Tours, and Tourism Information

Blue Owyhee Gems
blueowyheegems.com

Bob's Rock Shop
rockhounds.com

Geo-Tools Guided Field Trips
geo-tools.com/11-03.htm

Idaho Agates
agateswithinclusions.com

Idaho Rock Shop
idahorockshop.com

PaleoChick
paleochick.blogspot.com/2008/11/spence-gulch-trilobite-trip.html

Pebble Pup
pebblepup.com

Pierce Chamber of Commerce
pierce-weippechamber.com

Rare Rocks and Gems
rarerocksandgems.com

APPENDIX B: CLUBS

I strongly urge you to join your local club. The listings here are as accurate as possible, but because contacts change frequently, I left them out. Check the Northwest Federation of Mineralogical Societies web page (amfed.org/northwes.htm) for updated information.

Eureka Rock & Gem Club
Mountain Home, Idaho
Meetings: First Tuesday of each month at Mountain Home Senior Center

Geological Society of the Oregon Country (GSOC)
(Includes Washington, Oregon, and Idaho)
Portland, Oregon
Meetings: Second Friday of each month at Portland State University
gsoc.org

Gold Hill Diggers Gem & Mineral Club
Moscow, Idaho
Meetings: Second Sunday of each month at members' homes

Hells Canyon Gem Club, Inc.
Lewiston, Idaho
Meetings: Second Friday of each month at Lewis & Clark State College
hellscanyongemclub.com

Idaho Falls Gem & Mineral Society
Idaho Falls, Idaho
Meetings: Second Monday of each month at Idaho Falls Public Library

Idaho Gem Club, Inc.
Boise, Idaho
Meetings: Third Tuesday of each month at the Church of the Brethren, 2823 Cole Rd.

Intermountain Faceters Guild
Burley, Idaho
Meetings: First Saturday of January and every other month thereafter, as listed in OFF-The-Dop newsletter

Magic Valley Gem Club
Twin Falls, Idaho
Meetings: Third Thursday of each month at 235 Third Ave. East

North America Research Group (NARG)
(Fossil group; covers Washington, Oregon, Idaho, and British Columbia)
Hillsboro, Oregon
Meetings: First Wednesday of each month at Rice Museum
narg-online.com

North Idaho Mineral Club
Hayden, Idaho
Meetings: Third Thursday of each month at Lake City Senior Center, 1916 Lakewood Dr.
northidahomineralclub.org

Owyhee Gem & Mineral Club
Caldwell, Idaho
Meetings: Third Wednesday of each month at Albertson's College of Idaho, Boone Science Building

Petrified Watermelon Pickers
Jerome, Idaho
PO Box 402, King Hill, ID 83633

Southeast Idaho Gem & Mineral Society
Pocatello, Idaho
Meetings: Second Thursday of every month except June, July, and August at ISU Museum of Natural History
facebook.com/SEIGMS

Stallknecht-Morgan Museum Gem & Mineral Society
Letha, Idaho
Meetings: Last Wednesday of each month at 8491 West Idaho Blvd.

APPENDIX C: ROCK, GEM, AND PROSPECTING SHOPS

This list is based on internet searches, personal experience, and other sources. With luck these shops will be 100 percent internet accessible in the near future.

Anderson Rock Shop, 269 West Center St., Shelley, ID 83274; (208) 357-3348

Bob's Prospecting Supply, 1414 Ripon St., PO Box 671, Lewiston, ID 83501; (208) 743-3342

Devines Antiques & Rock Shop, Challis, ID 83226; (208) 879-2263

Driggs Plumbing & Rock Shop, 140 North Main St., Driggs, ID 83422; (208) 354-2562

Earth Lights Minerals & Gifts, 6481 Fairview Ave., Boise, ID 83706; (208) 373-7776

Gene's Rocks & Gems, 1824 South Kimball Ave., Caldwell, ID 83605-4827; (208) 459-1839

Gold Bar Mining Co., 101 Montgomery St., Idaho City, ID 83631; (208) 392-4597

Gold Dredge Builders Warehouse, HC69 Box 7, Riggins, ID 83549; (208) 628-3114; goldpanningtools.com/gold-guide/gold-dredge-builders-warehouse.htm

Idaho Prospecting Supply, 560 Third Ave., Wendell, ID 83355; (208) 536-4694

JR's Rock Shop, 1006 East Third Ave., Post Falls, ID 83854-9567; (208) 773-2474

Lemhi Rock Shop, 1155 Yellowstone Ave., Pocatello, ID 83201-4369; (208) 237-5273

Mac's Rock Shop, 3437 Taft St., Boise, ID 83703; (208) 345-6290

Miner's Shanty, 412 South Main St., Pierce, ID 83546; (208) 464-2704

Paul Rock Shop, 750 West 100 St., Paul, ID 83347-8636; (208) 438-5945

R and J's Creations and Rock Shop, 6055 Government Way, Ste. 5, Coeur d'Alene, ID 83815; (208) 762-4950

Rock Art, 904 Sixth St., PO Box 610, Clarkston, WA 99403; (509) 751-0956

Rock-N-Gifts, 942 South Lincoln St., Jerome, ID 83338; (208) 324-8860

Rose Hill Coins and Prospecting Supplies, 3506 Rose Hill, Boise, ID 83705; (208) 343-3220

Spirit Lake Rock Shop, 312 North Fifth Ave., Spirit Lake, ID 83869; (208) 623-2562

Stewart's Gem Shop, 2618 West Idaho St., Boise, ID 83702; (208) 342-1151

Stringer's Gem Shop, 1812 West Orchard Ave., Nampa, ID 83651; (208) 466-5169

Teton Jade and Gem, 140 North Main St., Driggs, ID 83422; (208) 354-2562

Triple A Rock Shop, 408 East Carol St., Nampa, ID 83687; (208) 461-3333 (shop), (208) 466-5706 (home); triplearockshop.com

BIBLIOGRAPHY

Adams, Mildrette. *Historic Silver City: The Story of the Owyhees.* Homedale, ID: Owyhee Publishing, 1999; 98 pgs.

Alt, David, and Donald W Hyndman. *Roadside Geology of Idaho.* Missoula, MT: Mountain Press Publishing Co., 1995; 393 pgs.

Ballard, Samuel M. "Geology and Gold Resources of Boise Basin, Boise County, Idaho," in *Idaho Bureau of Mines and Geology Bulletin* 9 (December 1924); 103 pgs.

Beckwith, John A. *Gem Minerals of Idaho.* Caldwell, ID: Caxton Printers, 1998; 129 pgs.

Campbell, Arthur. *Thirty-ninth Annual Report of the Mining Industry of Idaho, for the Year 1937.* Boise, ID: State of Idaho, 1938; 309 pgs.

Chesterman, Charles W. *The Audubon Society Field Guide to North American Rocks and Minerals.* New York: Alfred A. Knopf, 1979; 850 pgs.

DeLorme Idaho Atlas and Gazetteer. Yarmouth, ME: DeLorme Maps, 2000; 63 pgs.

Eckert, Allan W. *Earth Treasures, Volume 3: The Northwestern Quadrant.* New York: Harper & Row, 1987; 635 pgs.

Fanselow, Julie. *Idaho Off the Beaten Path.* Guilford, CT: Globe Pequot Press, 2006; 194 pgs.

Fisher, Tim. *Ore-Rock-On.* DVD, version 6.0. Sandy, OR, 2008.

Geological Society of the Oregon Country. *Golden Anniversary Campout: Lewiston, Idaho.* 1984; 80 pgs.

———. *President's Campout: Sawtooth Mountains and the Stanley Basin, Idaho.* 1978; 14 pgs.

Gold Prospectors Association of America. *GPAA Claims Club Membership Mining Guide.* Temecula, CA: GPAA, 2007; 504 pgs.

Hackbarth, Linda. *Bayview and Lakeview, and Other Early Settlements on Southern Lake Pen d'Oreille before 1940.* Coeur d'Alene, ID: Museum of North Idaho, 2003; 128 pgs.

Hendrickson, Borg, and Linwood Laughy. *Clearwater Country! The Traveler's Historical and Recreational Guide.* Kooskia, ID: Mountain Meadow Press, 1990; 171 pgs.

Hodges, Montana, and Robert Feldman. *Rockhounding Montana.* Guilford, CT: Globe Pequot Press, 2006; 239 pgs.

Idaho Road and Recreation Atlas. Medford, OR: Benchmark Maps, 2007; 95 pgs.

Johnson, H. Cyril. *Western Gem Hunters Atlas: Rock Locations from California to the Dakotas and British Columbia to Texas.* Susanville, CA: Cy Johnson & Son, 1998; 80 pgs.

Johnson, Robert Neil. *Gold Diggers Atlas.* Susanville, CA: Cy Johnson & Son, 1971; 64 pgs.

———. *N.W. Gem Fields and Ghost Town Atlas.* Susanville, CA: Cy Johnson & Son, 1969; 48 pgs.

Kaysing, Bill, and Ruth Kaysing. *Great Hot Springs of the West.* Santa Barbara, CA: Capra Press, 1993; 223 pgs.

Koschmann, A. H., and M. H. Bergendahl. *Principal Gold-Producing Districts of the United States.* US Geological Survey Professional Paper 610. Washington, DC: Government Printing Office, 1968; 283 pgs.

Lapidary Journal. *The Agates of North America.* San Diego, CA: Arts and Crafts Press, 1996; 96 pgs.

Litton, Evie. *Hiking Hot Springs in the Pacific Northwest.* Guilford, CT: Globe Pequot Press, 2001; 339 pgs.

Monaco, James Martin, and Jeanette Monaco. *Fee Mining and Rockhounding Adventures in the West.* Baldwin Park, CA: Gem Guides Book Co., 2002; 249 pgs.

Patera, Alan H. *Pacific Northwest Mining Camps, Western Places.* Lake Grove, OR: 1994; 66 pgs.

Preston, R. N., and M. L. Preston. *Idaho Gold and Gems Maps—Then and Now.* maps-nwd.com.

Ream, Lanny R. *The Gem & Mineral Collector's Guide to Idaho.* Baldwin Park, CA: Gem Guides Book Co., 2000; 79 pgs.

———. *Gem Trails of Idaho and Western Montana.* Baldwin Park, CA: Gem Guides Book Co., 2012; 256 pgs.

———. *Gems and Minerals of Washington.* Renton, WA: Jackson Mountain Press, 1994; 217 pgs.

———. *Idaho Minerals: The Complete Reference and Guide to the Minerals of Idaho.* Coeur d'Alene, ID: Museum of Northern Idaho, 2004; 373 pgs.

Romaine, Garret. *Gem Trails of Oregon.* Baldwin Park, CA: Gem Guides Book Co., 2009; 272 pgs.

———. *Gem Trails of Washington.* Baldwin Park, CA: Gem Guides Book Co., 2007; 200 pgs.

Sparling, Wayne. *Southern Idaho Ghost Towns.* Caldwell, ID: Caxton Printers, 1996; 135 pgs.

Thompson, Ida. *The Audubon Society Field Guide to North American Fossils.* New York: Alfred A. Knopf, 1992; 847 pgs.

Topographic Recreational Map of Idaho. Canon City, CO: GTR Mapping, 1999.

Tschernich, Rudy. *Zeolites of the World.* Phoenix, AZ: Geoscience Press, Inc., 1992; 565 pgs.

US Geological Survey. *Mineral Resources of the United States—Calendar Year 1907.* Washington, DC: Government Printing Office, 1908; 743 pgs.

Welch, Julia Conway. *Gold Town to Ghost Town: The Story of Silver City, Idaho.* Moscow, ID: University of Idaho Press, 1982; 124 pgs.

Wells, Merle W. *Gold Camps and Silver Cities: Nineteenth-Century Mining in Central and Southern Idaho.* Moscow, ID: University of Idaho Press, 2002; 233 pgs.

INDEX

ABOUT THE AUTHOR

Garret Romaine has been an avid rockhound, fossil hunter, and gold prospector since the 1970s. He began his writing career as a journalist, covering sports, environment, business, and technology in the Portland, Oregon, area. He switched to technical writing and won numerous awards developing computer manuals. Garret teaches technical writing at Portland State University and was named a Fellow in the Society for Technical Communication. He holds a bachelor's degree in geology from the University of Oregon and a master's degree in geography from the University of Washington, plus an MBA from Portland State University. His other titles for FalconGuides include *Gold Panning the Pacific Northwest, Gold Panning California, Rocks, Gems, and Minerals of the Rocky Mountains, Modern Rockhounding and Prospecting Handbook,* and *Basic Rockhounding and Prospecting: A Beginner's Guide.* He also wrote *Gem Trails of Oregon, Gem Trails of Washington, Gem Trails of Northern California,* and *Geology Lab for Kids.* He is currently the executive director for the Rice Northwest Museum of Rocks and Minerals in Hillsboro, Oregon.